No More Rejections

Get Published Today!

Penny C. Sansevieri

ISBN 0-7414-1111-3

For information contact:
Penny C. Sansevieri
Post Office Box 421156
San Diego, CA 92142
penny@booksbypen.com
www.nomorerejections.com

Text design & layout by Robert Goodman, Silvercat®, SanDiego, CA

To subscribe to our free Get Published! newsletter send e-mail to
Get-Published-subscribe@topica.com

Other books by Penny C. Sansevieri:

The Cliffhanger

Get Published! An author's guide to the on-line publishing revolution.

Published by:

519 West Lancaster Avenue
Haverford, PA 19041-1413
Info@buybooksontheweb.com
www.buybooksontheweb.com
Toll-free (877) BUY BOOK
Local Phone (610) 520-2500
Fax (610) 519-0261

Printed in the United States of America

Published January, 2003

Contents

Marketing, Not For The Faint At Heart

The dictionary is the only place that success comes before work.

ٶ Anonymous

Acknowledgments

There are many people I need to thank, so many in fact I almost don't know where to begin. Thanks to ALL of my colleagues who have given me feedback and assistance, the readers of the first edition of Get Published, and all of my newsletter subscribers who continue to go with me on this journey. To Jane whom I can not thank enough for her unwavering support of me, Joyce who not only believes in me but suffered through my "Titanic" phase. She deserves a medal for that one. To Melanie whose dedicated support of my writing has given me immense confidence, Franca who understands why I can't have a life….my writing is my life. To Kathleen who's words  "Here drink this and read this…" will go down as one of our most historical (or was it hysterical) moments. To Susan whose dedication and perseverance to her work are always an inspiration to me.

Thanks to all the writers who were willing to share their stories with me for the creation of this book.

Disclaimer

The criteria for being included in this book was simple. Publishers must have a standard of excellence that is unwavering. During the creation of *Get Published Today*, I purposefully excluded some publishers who I did not feel met those standards. My goal with this book was to pass along only those publishers I felt would keep the author's best interest at heart. While I have only personally worked with three of those included in this book, I thoroughly examined all of them. I researched and spoke with authors who published and promoted their book in this non-traditional manner as well as those who published through traditional publishing houses. There are more on-line resources, of course, and new ones arriving all the time. I find that in this industry, business models are constantly changing to make them more appealing and user friendly to the author. Contracts will change to adapt to the needs of the author. When there are updates, I will post those to my bi-weekly newsletter as well as to future editions of *Get Published Today*!

Foreword

First of all, let me say: Congratulations! You've started and maybe even finished a book. Do you have any idea what an amazing accomplishment that is? True, while you hear about the hundreds of thousands of people who write each year, think of all of those people you never hear anything about. All of those hundreds of thousands of stories that never get recognition or never even get finished. I, for one, sometimes forget the magnitude of this. We're all so busy climbing to the next level that we sometimes forget the level we're on and the triumph it is to even get this far. Take a moment to pat yourself on the back.

Now, let's get to work.

When I was a kid, I would dream of becoming a published author assuming it would bring with it immediate fame, fortune, a front row seat at the Oscars and a date with Nicolas Cage. As you can imagine, that didn't prove to be quite true. Still, this journey has been amazing and while it's been nothing that I thought it would be, it's been all that I could have hoped for. With the exception of the fame and fortune thing and oh yeah, Nic still won't return my calls.

Come with me on this journey while we learn and explore this fascinating new industry together and get you on the road to becoming a published author.

Introduction

*T*here are several ways to get your book published these days.

One way is to go the traditional route, submitting query letters to agents then waiting for their response. You could also self-publish, but that was often too costly and complicated a venture. It wasn't until about three years ago that another option began to present itself. That option is called on-line or on-demand publishing. Now, to alleviate some confusion let me say that we're not talking about e-books here (although that's also an option) we're talking about the real thing. The book you always dreamt of holding in your hand.

Before you turn up your nose to the idea of on-line publishing, consider this—the typical, big New York publisher prints about 800 titles a year. At last count, some of the on-line publishers were doing 500 a month. Early estimates indicate that on-line publishers printed around a half a million books in 2001. This year, there are indications that the on-line/epublishing industry will be about a $78 billion dollar market. These indicators tell us that the on-line publishers are growing at a pace no one ever anticipated. Why? Because they are filling a void in the industry. You want to get your book published? You want to begin to create a name for yourself? This is how you can do it.

Imagine this—you publish your first novel through one of these new on-line publishing companies, but you not only publish it, you can sell it too. And, you not only sell it, you sell it well. So well in fact, that you will either garner the attention from one of the traditional literary giants, or, when your second book is ready for submission to a publisher, you can include in your packet all the progress you made with your first book. Publishing companies like to see authors that are actively involved with their books. Because the truth is, they don't spend a whole lot of time with newbies. One fallacy among writers is that when you sign with a traditional publishing house, you no longer have to handle all of the promotion of the book yourself. Not true. The fact is that while it's nice to have the power that a well-known name brings, you can't expect to sit on your laurels and wait for the royalty checks to come in. In fact, publishing houses will usually promote you up to ninety days from the time of publication. If the book hasn't taken off by then, you're on your own. Some companies don't even promote first time authors that much unless the subject matter is such that it becomes a media bandwagon. In fact, did you know that when published traditionally, your book has the shelf life of milk? Forty-two days to be exact. If it's not flying off the bookstore shelves in forty-two days, it's headed to the remainder table, or, even worse, the shredder. Ever heard of a little book called: *Don't Sweat the Small Stuff?* Well, it was only discovered when it was sitting outside a bookstore by the dumpster. The story goes that someone in the publishing industry was walking past the dumpster, saw the books and the rest is history.

Despite some initial challenges, I am glad to have gone this route with my first book, *The Cliffhanger*. It has done exceedingly well, despite the negative biases surrounding this type of publishing and despite print-on-demand (which we will elaborate on later in this book). I have learned more than I ever thought I would. In fact, having spent some time dabbling in the industry with freelance work, writing an article here and there. I thought I knew everything. Boy, was I in for a surprise. This book is meant in no way to be the last book on publishing and marketing you will ever buy. In fact, I encourage you to stay constantly immersed in a variety of books on marketing as there are many great ones. It's important for you as a new author to be in a constant state of learning. You've spent years developing your talent as a writer. Now, it's time to develop another talent: your ability to market.

This book will introduce you the various publishers and the idea of print-on-demand and marketing these types of publications. I've gathered everything that I've learned, and now, I'm imparting it to you. Keep in mind that, like you, I am continuing to learn new things every day. While this information is as of this writing, current, things change, sometimes on a daily basis. My commitment to you is to keep this book as up-to-date as I can with frequent updates and additions. And if you see something in here that isn't quite right, or perhaps a web site that's out of date. E-mail me at penny@booksbypen.com.

1

On-Line Publishing: A Brief History

Where Did These "New" Publishers Come From?

With the odds stacked against them, authors were clamoring for some other way to get into this exclusive and sometimes unforgiving industry. Self-publishing worked well for a lot of people, but for most, it was too cost prohibitive. Costs for self-publishing can soar from $25,000 to $45,000 for a single book. A few on-line geniuses saw the potential in this and began to sense the possibilities an ever-expanding Internet had to offer. Several of them have been around since the inception of the World Wide Web; others, followed shortly thereafter. Some of these companies were founded by writers trying to break free from the confines of the traditional publishing cycle, while others were just a handful of people who saw the "phenomenon" potential in this business. Despite their differences, these companies have one thing in common; they are in a constant state of change. There is so much happening so quickly, that I think none of them expected the volume of writers that would beat a path to their virtual doors.

On getting rejection letters

I was certain they (publishers) were in cahoots and were sitting up nights trying to find reasons why they couldn't publish my book.

I got more excuses than you can imagine.

Janet Elaine Smith, *Dunnottar*

What Exactly Is On-Line Publishing?

Well, somewhere in between publishing the traditional way and self-publishing is what we call, the new on-line publishers. It's what I call, self-publishing with a twist. It used to be, if you wanted to circumvent the publishing houses, you had to take on everything from printers, to cover designers, ISBN numbers to distribution. Feeling dizzy yet? Sure, there are also self-publishing houses (called vanity presses). They churn out about 6,000 titles per year and the author pays anywhere from $10,000 to $20,000 to publish their book. That, in and of itself, was enough to discourage anyone who had not spent a great deal of time in the industry. It seemed the options were pretty limited, until the Internet explosion.

Then, enter the on-line publisher.

Essentially, what you're doing with the on-line publishers is hiring them to publish your work. You make the initial contact and have them send you a publishing kit (or in some instances you can view this entire kit on-line) which you can peruse at your leisure. Then, when you feel you're ready, begin exploring their web site and start your publishing process.

Most of the work is done via the publisher's web site. There are a myriad of places to get your questions answered and when you're ready, you can upload your file, inputting all of the pertinent information such as an author bio, back matter or back flap information, etc. And, while the process may seem very clinical, it's really quite thorough.

Do not be hasty when filling out this form. I was so excited when I began this process that I quickly began entering information. Luckily, I stopped myself before I got to the point of no return. Consider this—the information that you put in there will somehow, somewhere, land up on your book. Take your time. Visit a bookstore and look up books in your genre. This will give you an idea of what works. Don't copy, but learn. Learn from the pros, those authors that have gone before you. Then, when you're ready, fire up that computer and begin your publishing process.

When I started entering my information for *The Cliffhanger*, I did it in steps. It took me about eight nights to get it all entered and exactly the way I wanted it. Every site is set up differently, but there is always the opportunity to make changes before it's too late. Better safe than sorry. Although, I have to warn you, I'm a little bit more anal than most. It probably won't take you eight nights to do this. Most other non-anal types can probably do it in four.

Now, don't be afraid to contact them personally. I know a lot of people are leery about contacting a real person when so much interaction is encouraged on-line, but trust me when I say they expect it. In fact, most even encourage it.

When I began toying with the idea of having iUniverse. com publish *The Cliffhanger*, I researched them thoroughly. You don't want to go into something like this blindly, and if you're serious about staying in the business for a long time, you want to make sure that whoever is handling your first manuscript will treat it like it is their own. I tell you, I contacted them so much over the telephone that I began knowing the customer service agents by name. It was really beneficial for me to do this and it also helped me feel more secure that they really did know what they were talking about. Depending on what your specific needs are, the criteria for what makes a good on-line publishing company vary. For some, it's the turn around time, for others it's whether or not they can print in hardcover. Generally though, you first and foremost want a quality product. "The first thing I'd recommend looking for is book production quality." suggests Pam Hansell former self-publishing Editor of *Inkspot*. "Distribution time is the second element I'd look into when selecting an on-line publisher. To research both of these elements I'd suggest spending some time on the company's web site. Visit their on-line bookstore, choose a book or two, and place an order. This will accomplish two things—you'll see firsthand how long it takes the book to reach you, rather than how long the company says the book will take, and you'll also be able to examine the product. Check out the print quality on the cover and interior pages. See if the binding is secure. You're paying for this product so it helps to see what the end result is."

> I really hate the term "vanity press."
> Anyone who has spent any time at all marketing a POD books knows there's nothing vain about it.
> Penny C. Sansevieri, *Get Published Today!*

❧

How They Make This Work

You're probably wondering what the catch is, aren't you? Well, of course, there's always a catch, as they say. And while I'm not sure that this is a reason for you to launch into skeptic-mode, there are a number of things to consider. First and foremost, what makes it possible for these companies to offer this type of a service to you is because of a little something called POD, or print-on-demand. Print-on-demand is exactly that. Books are printed as they are needed. This means there is no first run and no overrun and someone (probably you) will not be stuck with 10,000 books if they don't sell. Now, while this may seem all hearts and flowers to you right now, there are a few things to consider. First of all, as of this writing, print-on-demand is still a printing process that is vying for acceptance. One of the biggest issues with print-on-demand is that there is no return policy in place for these POD books. The fact of the matter is that people return merchandise. And I know it sends shivers up your spine to think that someone will not like your book enough and want to return it. Take heart. The return ratio averaged from 10% to 25% in 1995 and then escalated to a whopping 35% in 1997. This is not a personal issue; it's a matter of fact. Americans love to be able to return things. You'd never get away with this in any country other than America. If you're marketing for Europe, you'll make a fortune. For now, though, the return rate is something to keep in mind.

Now, these return figures that I've stated above are strictly for bookstores. Warehouse stores (such as the Costco) are much higher and most times, when items are returned at these warehouse stores, they're usually in pretty bad shape. But they continue to accept these returns back into their stores because their vendors want "in" so badly that they will accept their fair share of unsaleable product back in stock just to keep their inventory and their presence in these high-volume stores.

If you have aspirations of these on-line giants launching some sort of marketing campaign, you can forget it. While some of these companies do offer marketing assistance, even press release design, none of them will promise to manage your marketing campaign for you. One reason for this is, that they are cranking out some 500 books a day and it would be impossible for them to have their hands in each and every marketing plan. When it comes to getting your book out there, the responsibility rests firmly on your shoulders. Or that of your publicist, if you should decide to hire one.

Can POD Work For You?

Sure it can. New authors make it work every day. The beauty of print-on-demand is that your book will never go out of print. You may run a marketing campaign that sends it to the best seller list this year and then two years from now (after you're rich and famous) decide that it's got some more life left in it and begin marketing it again. One of the great things about this is that with print-on-demand, you can easily (and fairly inexpensively) test market a book or idea before putting a big-bucks marketing campaign behind it. Also the hope is, and always will remain, that as often as we complain about traditional publishers, we'd love to get picked up by one. And it does happen. It happens more than we realize. The thing is, by the time the book gets republished under a new publishing company, everyone has long since forgotten where it originated and that's a shame. Now, print-on-demand might not work if you have your heart set on seeing your book in every single bookstore in the country. The reasons for this again go back to the return issue. But, that said, you're not publishing traditionally so don't get caught up in focusing solely on traditional markets.

What You Get In Return

Now, you are probably wondering what you get in return for all of your hard work. Well, you get a book. And believe me when I say, that the moment you hold your book in your hand is an experience you will never forget. I cried, I screamed, I called my mother. It's big. Bigger than you can imagine. But don't let the whole first-time author thing blind you to your choice. I reiterate, (and will continue to do so throughout this book, sometimes ad nauseum so bear with me) don't settle for anything less than what you really want. If on-line or self-publishing is not for you, then by all means, continue traditionally. But if you believe enough in yourself and in your work that you feel you can not only get it published, but sell it, then read on.

Did you know?

A self-published success story: Irma Rombauer spent $3,000 to put together a little recipe book to assist families who cooked at home. Guess what it was called…
The Joy of Cooking.

I'm all in favor of keeping dangerous weapons out of the hands of fools. Let's start with typewriters.

✷ Frank Lloyd Wright, 1868–1959

2

Are You Ready To Be An Author?

$\mathcal{P}$lease take a few moments to answer the following questions:

- Why do I want to write a book?

- Do I know how much my book will cost to produce?

- Who will buy my book?

- How much do I think they will be willing to pay for my book?

- Do I have a passion for my work and will others feel my passion?

- Can I wear the many hats of an entrepreneur?

- Can I engage others to help me produce and sell my books?

- Am I too proud to ask for help?

- Am I willing to spend years promoting my book?

- How can I make my book different from others already published on my subject?

- Can I set clear goals and follow a plan?

One of the best assets anyone can have is knowing their limitations. Now, I don't mean this in a derogatory sense. But face it, we all have them. Knowing what they are and dealing with them in advance, will put us a step ahead of the process. Not acknowledging them and not dealing with them will take away precious time and energy from your project. Answering these questions will be a real eye opener for most. Honest answers will indicate areas that you really need to focus on. And, through this focus, help you get as much out of this book as you can. Then, when you're done reading this book, go back and answer them again and see how you do. I'm certain that you'll be amazed at your progress.

The Publishers!

A journey of a thousand miles begins
with a single step.

❧ Confucius

3

Let's Begin

*W*hen the first edition came out of Get Published!, several of the companies I interviewed implemented new contracts and additions to their existing services. The fact of the matter is, these publishers will change. The life of an on-line publisher changes almost daily. Some companies have started with the best of intentions, yet seen their hopes and dreams vanish in a fog of sheer "overwhelm." The truth is, the demand is so great for these publishers that, as the song goes, "only the strong survive." And even then, I found their services changing so fast; it was often difficult to keep up with them all. The companies that want to make it big in the publishing world realize that they must be in a constant state of adaptation. Some companies are even so cautious that they will readily admit, what is today, might not be tomorrow. If the demand is there, they will make it happen for the author. Their success depends on your success.

Also, keep in mind that while I tried to give each publisher equal time, some have more to offer than others do. It's just a fact. Regardless of my personal publishing choices, I do not endorse one publisher over another. Largely because what one company offers might be perfect for my book but less than perfect for yours.

Now, let's get down to some of the nitty-gritty things you should be looking for.

First of all, it's important to note that book prices vary considerably depending on the length of the book, genre, etc. I've tried to get as close to the mark as I can on book prices because this will become a very integral part of your marketing plan. As a first-time author, you do not want a book that is overpriced, making it very tough to sell. And while some bookstores will disagree with me, I found one of my biggest stumbling blocks initially was the price of my book. Once I built a reputation for myself and the stores knew my books would sell, this became a non-issue. But better to not have to overcome that along with everything else while you're marketing your masterpiece.

Another thing to keep in mind while reviewing these publishers is whether or not they list with Ingram*. I found that my listing with Ingram really helped to boost my sales. Largely due to the fact that a lot of bookstores I spoke with will stock a book only if it's listed on the Ingram distribution list. Some publishers balk at this and some don't even list with Ingram. They give you the option of submitting the listing yourself, if you get your own ISBN number (getting your own ISBN means handling your own distribution). As we'll discuss later in this book, bookstores might not be your best primary consideration for your book. That said, having the option to get a bookstore to carry them is still worth its weight in gold. One of the primary reasons I found that on-line publishers don't list with Ingram is that they don't want to fork over the percentage Ingram demands for a coveted listing in their catalog. I say, weigh your options and see what will best benefit you and your book sales.

A listing with *Books in Print* is another great advantage to you. *Books in Print* is essentially a database of books available for pur-

---

*Ingram is one of the largest book distributors in the United States. Their database of books is linked to most bookstores around the country.

chase. If you opt not to list with Ingram, some stores might still consider stocking your book as long as you have a listing with *Books in Print* (check out their Web site at booksinprint.com). Although I have never tried to obtain a listing there myself, I'm told that it's fairly painless and entirely free of charge.

One of the things these publishers are also beginning to offer are marketing packages. I've tried most of them and what I didn't try, I interviewed authors who did. While these packages are put together with the best of intentions but they are largely ineffective to most authors. Why? Because the author assumes that one package purchased is all it will take to get his or her book noticed. That's simply not true. You can purchase all the marketing packages in the world but they will fall short of your expectations if you do not follow up. A fax blast package, for example, is only as effective as the follow up you do. When you're shopping marketing plans, know that even if your press release is sent to three hundred people in the media, two hundred of them might not be qualified buyers. To give you an example of what I mean let me tell you the story of an author who came to see me about her book. She had purchased a press kit package, which included faxing her press release to seven hundred media contacts around the country. Now, you might think: Wow! That's really a great start. But more is not necessarily better. Sometimes it's just more. I asked her to see if she could get the list of people her press release was sent to. She requested it from her publisher and it was sent over almost immediately. When I got the list I noticed there were editors on there from every national magazine in the country, including: *Biker's Monthly, Car and Driver,* and *Equestrian Monthly.* This would have been fine except that her book was a romance novel that had nothing to do with any of the above publications. The likelihood of them mentioning her book was probably nil. As a matter of fact, what you'll end up doing is getting a reputation of sending out useless releases. And don't think I'm kidding. Those in the media share all kinds of information with each other. Send them a useless lead and sooner or later you'll find it limits your potential for any future coverage. To give you an example of this, I recently had lunch with an editor who told me she gets about 200 faxes each day from a particular on-line publisher who sells a fax blasting program to their authors. She said she gets so many of them she has told her staff to discard anything coming from this publisher. She said they're not only poorly written but often don't match the demographic of her magazine.

My advice to you is get the marketing packages if you want them, but understand that you must do the necessary follow-up. If you decide to have your press release faxed around the country, get a list of potential recipients before you commit to a package. If they're unwilling to give that to you, then find someone else who will. You're far better off contacting twenty topic-related contacts than two hundred random names.

When a musician puts out his own CD, no one says, "Hey, what' the matter? You couldn't get a contract with CBS/Sony?" No, he is lauded for it. When a filmmaker maxes out his or her credit cards to make their own movie, does someone say, "Oh, I guess this movie is terrible; it wasn't put out by Miramax." No, the filmmaker is considered hip, cool, and creative. But when a writer self-publishes it's just a result of his or her own vanity right? I mean that's why they call it vanity press, right?

Wendy Tokunaga, *No Kidding—A Novel*

1ˢᵗ*Books Library*

Patrick East of 1stBooks Library says that despite the fact that they've been in business for only four years, they've managed to garner quite a bit of media attention. And while they don't offer a huge array of choices when it comes to publishing packages, what they do give you is quite substantial. A $399 set-up fee gets you in the door. From there you can opt to go with their trade paperback package at $199 or their hardcover option which is an additional $350. Check with them first though because they've been running a lot of specials recently at some very enticing prices. Both of these options come with the standard Ingram distribution as well as a listing with *Books in Print*, and an ISBN number. Both also pay a standard 30% royalty and offer a 30% discount on author purchases. Their statements are sent quarterly.

1st Books was one of the first companies to offer promotional packages. While they have offered a myriad of promotional choices in varying degrees of affordability, these packages proved largely ineffective. It is my understanding that 1st Books is looking to do away with them. I actually purchased some of their packages to "test market" them and was surprisingly disappointed. I believe their packages became so popular with new authors that they were ill-equipped to handle the volume. Suffice it to say, 1st Books strongest advantage is their highly successful publishing structure and affordability to the author.

Contact Information:
1stBooks Library
www.1stbooks.com
(800) 839-8640

1stBooks Library		Comments
Package price	$399 initial fee–$199 for softcover–additional $350 for hardback.	
Distribution	Ingram	
Retail book price	Typically $17.10	
Rights	Remain with author	
Royalty	30%	
Author discounts	30%	
Time from manuscript to book	3 to 6 months	
24/7 Sales tracker	Yes	
Page min/max	108 min/740 max	
Approval process	None	
Hard/softcover	Both	
Listing with *Books in Print*	Yes	
Royalties paid	Quarterly	
Cancellation	Author can cancel at anytime	

Booklocker.com

For a $199 set-up fee a writer can submit their book to Booklocker.com and four to six weeks later have the finished product in their mailbox. This is a fairly up-front service about what they will and won't accept. And, like several other on-line publishers, they've had authors that have been accepted through traditional publishing houses.

With Booklocker.com, you can choose to let them obtain your ISBN for you or you can obtain your own number. Regardless of who owns the ISBN, they will still list you with Ingram and all major bookstores (both on-line and brick and mortar stores).

After having spent a good deal of time researching them, it's apparent that they try to keep their services as simple as possible. They have a no-questions asked, same-day cancellation policy and since they handle their printing in-house can turn a book order around in 48 hours. They also offer an on-line promo kit to authors publishing through them which assists the author with submitting to search engines and on-line discussion lists. The author also determines pricing of the book, which is a nice incentive since you can decide your price based on the market you wish to target.

Located in Bangor, Maine, Booklocker is available only via E-mail and does not print their phone number anywhere, nor do they encourage authors to call them. They are very up front about this. They work exclusively through E-mail (Angela Hoy says this is because they work with more then seven hundred authors at one time) and always responded within an hour to any request I sent.

Contact Information:
www.booklocker.com
Angela@booklocker.com

Booklocker		Comments
Package Price	$199	
Distribution	Ingram	
Retail book price	$11.95 min for 100 page book. Retail price increases with page count. No maximum price indicated	
Rights	Remain with author	
Royalty	35% for Booklocker site sales; 15% for wholesale to book-stores	
Author discounts	35%–60% depending on order quantity	
Time from manu-script to book	Four to six weeks	
Page min/max	100 page min 700 page max	
Approval process	Yes	
24/7 Sales tracker	Yes	
Hard/softcover	Hard and Softcover	
Listing with *Books in Print*	Yes	
Royalties paid	Monthly	
Cancellation	Same day	

eNovel

It's an exciting time at eNovel, according to its Chief Operating Officer, Alex Papajohn. They're revising their business model and creating a very author-friendly place to get published. They deal with both traditional publishing houses as well as aspiring authors and seem eager to conform their business to the needs of the masses. Alex Papajohn stated to me that eNovel does not charge a fee. This, he said, is to separate themselves from the vanity presses. If, however, an author decides not to use eNovel's free publishing system, the company offers fee-based author services too. Those services enable an author to get published in e-Book format, in print or as an audio book.

One of the things that struck me when talking with Alex, is that they are eager to make this work for the author. But, he stated, they also want to be realistic. Currently, if you chose to publish through eNovel, they will print your book in e-book format, meaning that it's not in trade paperback or hard cover. Then, the book goes on their site. If the authors book rises in the rankings into the Top Ten and stays there for a reasonable amount of time, it gets put into print-on-demand format and your book is ready for marketing to readers, editors and even traditional publishers. One reason they do this, says Papajohn, is to let the consumer decide what's going to sell. In my opinion, since they don't charge for their services, it would be easy for them to get inundated with books. If you're thinking of test marketing your book, this is a way you can let the public decide if it's print worthy or not. They'll leave your book up for one year. This is the current time frame and if after a year your book fails to sell more than a few copies, your agreement is canceled.

What I really enjoyed hearing about was the author account page. This is where you can track the sales of your book any time you feel the need to see how sales are going. This is a great option, in my opinion, and something every author should be concerned about.

They do offer a fairly complete package for their no-charge-publishing fee. Here's what it includes:

- Electronic publication of your book
- Standard book cover template
- Standard interior template
- They will help make your print book available on Amazon.com
- Distribution through other future Web-based retail and portal partners
- Publication of synopsis of book and author biography written by the author
- Publication of author photo (if available)
- Publication of first section of book for public to sample
- ISBN number
- 50% royalties on sale of book in both electronic and print-on-demand formats
- Customized author account page
- Publication of graphics, tables and pictures as part of your book (whether they are part of the text or the cover)

This entire process, he says, takes only four weeks, although it can take longer depending on how many books are being submitted at a given time.

I've spoken to Alex now several times and while I was a bit hesitant to include them in this book because of their still-developing business model. I felt that they deserved a mention because of the uniqueness of their services. They are trying to adapt their services specifically to the needs of the authors and are open to reasonable suggestions and ideas that will help to enhance their services. If you decide to publish through them, I'd appreciate you letting me know what your experience is. Feel free to E-mail me about this.

Contact Information:
eNovel
www.enovel.com
Keyword "Novel" on AOL
(804) 673-6111

eNovel Publishing		Comments
Package Price	$0-$250.00	Cover design additional
Distribution	Ingram	
Retail book price	$12.00 to $15.00	
Rights	Remain with author with the exception of electronic rights	
Royalty	50%	
Author discounts	No set policy. Offers volume discounts	
Time from manuscript to book	Four to six weeks	
Page min/max	108 min 750 max	
Approval process	Determined by ten random readers over a period of one year	
Hard/softcover	Softcover	
24/7 Sales tracker	Yes	
Listing with *Books in Print*	No	
Royalties paid	Semi-annual	
Cancellation	Not specified	They will consider canceling their agreement if author has grounds to do so. Double check with them before signing your contract.

Infinity Publishing

According to John Harnish, Director of Special Projects and Author's Advocate at Infinity Publishing, they've got one of the most flexible packages out there. For starters, their page minimum is only eighteen, opening the doors to authors who might not wish to publish something the length of War & Peace. Of course, if you do have something that ambitious, it's not a problem either. Their maximum book length is 750 pages. Furthermore, he says they own their own printing facility and are able to turn finished books around in 24 to 48 hours.

Part of their plan is to offer a great bookstore as well as a publishing center in one neat little package. One thing I found particularly appealing about Infinity Publishing is that they offer a 10% royalty on author purchases. Something no other company offers. "We feel that the best marketing tool is the book itself," says John, "that's why we not only offer a steep discount on these purchases, but offer a royalty fee as well."

Other royalty payments depend on where the book is purchased. If it's bought directly from their site, the author will get a 20% royalty. If it's purchased from another on-line store, or from a bookstore itself, the author gets 10%.

Author purchases are 50% off of the first order and 40% off of every order after that. For a one time set-up fee of $400, you get an ISBN number, a barcode, a formatted book for print-on-demand, a hard copy proof, submission to on-line e-tailers (Amazon and Barnes & Noble), a book cover design and Web pages about the book which are hosted on their e-commerce site (buybooksontheweb.com). Like most on-line publishers, Infinity offers up its share of marketing packages. Their packages are basic and are structured to give the author a jump start on their campaign. All of their packages include the creation of a press release, copies of your book, postcards, business cards, and bookmarks.

Their objective is to create one press release that the author can send out to media, bookstores, or on-line communities. The packages aren't meant to replace an author's campaign but rather enhance it.

During any given year, Infinity usually schedules several author conferences, seminars, and teleclasses. This variety of educational resources is offered to their authors to help them connect with other writers, further their success, and better understand the industry they're in.

Contact Information:
Infinity Publishing
www.inifinitypublishing.com
(877) 289-2665

INFINITY PUBLISHING		Comments
Package Price	$400	
Distribution	Ingram; Baker Taylor	
Retail book price	8.95 to 24.95	
Rights	Remain with author	
Royalty	20% on books bought directly from their site—10% when they sell books via book-stores	Pays author royalty on author purchases of 10%
Author discounts	50% off of first order; 40% off every other order	
Time from manu-script to book	Six weeks	
Page min/max	18 page min 750 page max	
Approval process	None	
24/7 Sales tracker	No	
Hard/softcover	Softcover	Plans to eventually offer both
Listing with *Books in Print*	Yes	
Royalties paid	Monthly	
Cancellation	Author can cancel at any time.	

iUniverse

iUniverse has gone through many changes since they opened their doors in 1996, but one thing has remained a constant: they want to see you get published. With a renovated web site, updated author contract and a slew of new services, they're doing what they can to revolutionize the business of on-line publishing. According to Doug Bennett, President and Chief Operating Officer, they have help 8,600 authors get published. Currently they're carrying about 10,000 titles and expect to see a double digit growth in business adding another 7,000 to 9,000 titles this year alone. They have struck partnerships with Adobe, IDG Books (the "For Dummies" collection), and Barnes & Noble. It's worth noting here that Barnes & Noble owns 49% of iUniverse but much like the Xlibris/Random House venture (see Xlibris chapter for more information on this), this doesn't mean an automatic "in" at your local Barnes & Noble store.

Their turn-around time has varied, but usually takes about six weeks to two months. This is a huge change from where they were two years ago. In fact, I can remember authors waiting six months to get their finished product. Their standard package begins at $159 and goes up from there. Their $159 package price though is for manuscripts submitted on-line. If you decide to mail your submission, the package price goes up to $259. Their packages are basic, but include everything you need to get your book published. It's very much a no frills kind of a thing. You get a book and you get a cover design; after that, you're on your own. Also, you're allowed up to twenty-five corrections on your manuscript before final production. This means that if you get your initial book back for proofing and find that you left some errors in it, there's still time to correct them. You also get to offer cover suggestions, or send them a cover photo (300 dpi). Their designers will take it from there.

Their approval processes are minimal. Approvals are essentially making sure that your manuscript is in a format they can use. You can download an approved format from their web site and then upload or E-mail your manuscript to them once the necessary chapter breaks are included. Once your manuscript is approved, you get assigned a publishing agent who will walk you through the process. Now, unlike some of their competitors, they do not get involved in the marketing process at all. They do offer some great information on their web site (see: Author Toolkit) that you're free to peruse and download as needed. They also offer educational services, and, you can join their extensive iUniverse community.

It's worth noting as well that your agreement with iUniverse is three years from the date of signing. You can cancel with a thirty-day notice, but iUniverse reserves the right to continue selling your book for twelve months after cancellation of your contract. Depending on the reason for your cancellation this could be a good or bad thing. If you decide to republish through someone else, you'll get a new ISBN number. Any straggler orders will still be able to get filled under the old ISBN number if they come in during the twelve-month time frame.

Their author discounts will vary depending on the purchase price of your book, but they begin at about 20% and go up to 35% depending on the amount of books you purchase. If you are purchasing your books from them related to an event, I highly encourage you to let the bookstore or venue handle the purchasing if at all possible. The reason for this is simple: You don't get royalties for author purchases.

As of this writing, iUniverse is in the process of setting up an author sales tracking page. In the interim, if you publish with them and need to check your royalty status you can e-mail their royalty department at royalties@iuniverse.com.

Contact Information:
iUniverse.com
www.iuniverse.com
(877) 823-9235

IUNIVERSE		Comments
Package Price	Begins at $159	$259 if you mail in your manuscript
Distribution	Ingram	
Retail book price	Prices begin at $9.95 but the average price is $16.00 to $20.95	
Rights	Electronic rights remain with author	
Royalty	20%	
Author discounts	Begin at 20% and go up to 35%	
Time from manuscript to book	Six weeks to two months	
Page min/max	108 page min 740 page max	
24/7 Sales tracker	Coming soon	
Approval process	None	
Hard/softcover	Soft	
Listing with *Books in Print*	Yes	
Royalties paid	Quarterly	
Cancellation	Author signs a three-year agreement, but can cancel this with a thirty-day notice. Publisher reserves the right to continue sale of the book for another year following the cancellation.	

PageFree Publishing

PageFree Publishing is the new kid on the block. Well, as new kids go these days. While they've been in business since 1998, they have recently begun making strides to claim their spot in the on-line publishing world. When I spoke with Kim Blagg, President of PageFree Publishing, she says she has spent most of her life in the publishing world and has seen many new ideas come and go. "This form of publishing," says Blagg, "is here to say." And that it is. PageFree recently underwent an entire revamp on their web site making it much easier to navigate and very user friendly.

When I interviewed Kim, she was very clear about the fact that she does everything she can to offer the best services to her authors. Their royalty is 75% of the net price and here's how that works. Say your book is set at the list price of $20.00 and you offer a 20% discount to the wholesaler, the wholesale price would be $16.00. Subtract the cost of printing the book, and your royalty is 75% of the difference.

Your manuscript is formatted in one of their standard templates; you are allowed up to three black and white interior photos and ten author line corrections. Your book will be made available as Print on Demand through Ingram Distribution, Baker & Taylor, bn.com, borders.com, amazon.com and thegreatamerican bookstore.com and *Books in Print*. There is a one-year archival fee (archival fee for additional years is $15.00). This archival fee keeps the books current in their listings. Most publishers don't require this, and it's likely PageFree will eventually do away with the archival fee altogether.

Contact Information:
PageFree Publishing
www.pagefreepublishing.com
(888) 707-7634

PageFree Publishing		Comments
Package Price	$299-$452	Priced by word—also $15 archival fee per year after the first year
Distribution	Ingram	
Retail book price	Author prices books	
Rights	Stay with the author	
Royalty	75% of net price	Net price is: whole-sale discount minus book print cost
Author discounts	Authors costs are: .17 cents per page plus $1.00 for cover	
Time from manu-script to book	Four to six weeks	
Page min/max	108 page min 740 page max	
Approval process	None	
Hard/softcover	Hard and soft cover	Dust covers are an additional $80.00 (one time fee)
Royalties paid	Quarterly	
24/7 Sales tracker	Not in place yet	
Listing with *Books in Print*	Yes	
Cancellation	Either party can can-cel this agreement at any time	

Trafford Publishing

It's apparent when you speak to anyone at Trafford that what they do is more than a job; it's a passion. One of the things I found interesting is that even their CEO, Bruce Batchelor, is an author. Their focus is the author, says Bruce, and who better to know and understand their needs than a fellow author? That's why Trafford hires writers and others with publishing industry experience wherever possible for all its author-contact positions. "It's a lot easier to understand their needs when they mirror your own," says Bachelor. Their programs are structured much differently from their counterparts. Some authors like Chris Lear, author of *Running with the Buffaloes*, like it that way, "It gave me the creative control I wanted, I knew exactly how the book was supposed to look and I was allowed to make it exactly that."

It's also worth noting that unlike their on-line counterparts, Trafford does only minimal cover design (two hours) and does not handle the interior layout of the book. This is solely up to the author. Despite the higher-priced programs and do-it-yourself service, their final product, says their CEO, will exceed the author's expectations each time.

When you contact Trafford, they will send you a publishing kit. This consists of a well thought out book, geared to answer any question you could possibly have, and a few you never even thought of.

Their packages begin at $499 and go up to $990. When I checked with Trafford for the latest edition of this book, they were charging a quarterly renewal fee. This fee has since been removed. While still minimal (fees ranged from $15 to $30 a quarter), it was a good marketing strategy to discontinue them. The services they offered for that fee are still in place. These services include:

- Keeping listings with the big on-line retailers working
- Maintaining their own e-commerce bookstore
- Bookkeeping and sending out quarterly royalty checks
- Archiving the print files and ensuring that the files are updated whenever the printer software is revised
- Updating the book's Web page to reflect excerpts from favorable reviews
- Answering inquiries from the authors themselves and updating their contact information.

Upon closer inspection of their packages, it would seem that an author looking to promote their book would only want to purchase their Best Seller package. Not just because it offers an attractive promotion package, but because it is only with this package that will get you listed with Amazon, Borders and Barnes & Noble, as well as *Books in Print*. All other packages require that you handle this process yourself. Also, the promotional package includes sending your news release to over 7,000 media contacts, submitting your Web page to over 800 search engines, 10,000 media contacts, 250 book announcement cards and nine free copies of your book. As far as the press releases go, the Trafford staff will not write these for you but they will provide comments and suggestions to the author on his or her draft of the release. Once the author has approved the final wording and the timing for release, Trafford staff will distribute it via E-mail to media contacts and to the author's own E-mail address. A printed copy will also be mailed to the author.

Trafford encourages authors to handle the distribution for their book themselves. Their Legacy Package ($499) and their Entrepreneur Package ($679) do not offer distribution to outside booksellers, although the Entrepreneur package does handle sales from the Trafford site.

At Trafford, it is the author who decides the retail price and, in so doing, establishes the royalty amount. First, Trafford calculates the single-copy printing cost for the book that is based on production factors (number of pages, type of paper, type of covers, binding, etc.). Next, the author decides the retail price based on his or her appraisal of the target audience. They recommend a retail price at least 2.5 times the single-copy printing costs to allow for an ample royalty.

As far as discounts go for author purchases, this is easily calculated based on the chart in the back of their publishing guide. The author only pays the cost of printing and this printing cost will decrease based on the number of copies purchased.

Trafford does not list through Ingram, largely because they feel the money they would commission back to Ingram is better off being sent to the author. Most of you, I'm sure, would agree. But keep in mind that to be considered by a bookstore, a listing with Ingram is a necessary part of the process. Instead though, they do offer a listing through Baker & Taylor Book Distributors (the US's second largest book distributor).

As far as author sales tracking goes, Trafford has a unique system in place to help authors gauge how effective their marketing efforts are. When a Trafford author logs onto their system they can not only track their sales, but they can also track these efforts by a particular zip code and city. As you're promoting your book, doing radio and television interviews or niche marketing, you'll be able to get good idea by market segment how well your efforts are paying off.

Trafford has offices in Victoria, B.C., Canada and in New Bern, North Carolina, USA. They were the first company to offer the on-demand publishing service (back in 1995) and currently serve authors from over two dozen countries.

Contact Information:
   Trafford Publishing
   www.trafford.com
   (888) 232-4444

Trafford Publishing		Comments
Package Price	Starts at $499	
Distribution	In-house	
Retail book price	$11.95 min $20.00 + max	
Rights	Remain with author	
Royalty	60% of gross margin	
Author discounts	Pays print cost	
Time from manu-script to book	4 to 6 weeks	
Page min/max	Page min 50 Page max 700	Coil bound books can be any page number
Approval process	None	
24/7 Sales tracker	Yes	Author can track sales by city
Hard/softcover	Soft only	
Listing with *Books in Print*	Yes (with larger package)	
Royalties paid	Quarterly	
Cancellation	Anytime	

Xlibris

Xlibris carries over 7,000 titles and sold over a quarter of a million books in 2001 alone. That, according to Director of Marketing, Joseph Keslar, far exceeded anyone's expectations. When they opened in 1997 they were printing 500 books a year. In 2002 that number quickly increased to 4,000. This number continues to escalate. It's a trend that is not only here to stay but one that is breaking any and all barriers that writers have previously known.

Their web site is simple and easy to navigate. There are also several resources for authors looking to enter the magazine submission arena as well as a listing of writer's workshops and conferences around the country.

One of the things that was evident when I interviewed them is, they are there for the author. Not just to help them get published, but to help them become successfully published. While they do not assist in any book marketing nor have any desire to offer those services, they do have a lot of areas where authors can seek assistance or connect with other Xlibris authors. They have a number of author communities that offer advice, assistance and a chance to "meet" other authors who have recently published as well. While Xlibris works very hard for the author, the company has not been without its challenges. In 2001 they sent a letter to 20,000 literary agents around the country encouraging them to get rid of their slush pile. The letter stated: "You've heard the saying one man's trash is another man's treasure? Now, find out how your slush pile can actually become a source of revenue...." Literary agents balked at this letter complaining about the ethics of taking a ten percent fee for sending rejected authors to Xlibris. A week later (and amidst a slew of apologies) the project was scrapped.

Xlibris has a series of packages, beginning with the basic service at $500. While each package is distinctively different, there are a series of essentials that stay constant in each. Included in all packages are the following items:

- Book Formatting
- Book Formats: trade paperback and e-book (Adobe Acrobat e-Book Reader)
- ISBN Numbers and UPC Barcode Registration with: amazon.com, borders.com, barnesandnoble.com, Ingram, *Books in Print*, and more than 200 on-line stores
- Electronic Galleys Paperback Royalties: 25% of cover price (direct sales), 10% (Distributor/Reseller sales)
- Author Discounts of 40% on Trade Paperbacks
- A public Author Web Page
- A Public Book Web Page
- Control over your Book Excerpt Viewable in Xlibris' On-line Bookstore
- On-line Book Sales Reporting
- Custom Book URL Registration

Each package is structured to fit every writer's needs. From the author who wants little control over their work, to those who want to have complete control. Their once free Core Package has been removed and all of their packages have been revamped. The basic package is $500 and includes the items listed on the bullet points above. You have the option to purchase a slew of add-ons as well, but if you're going to make that many additions to the original package, you're probably better off stepping up to their Professional Service Package ($900) or their Custom Service Package at $1600. While this last one seemed initially a bit pricey to me, it quite literally comes with just about everything.

One of the nice things about Xlibris is their add-ons. As I mentioned above, if you're going to add a lot of items to their Basic Package you're probably better off upgrading. If, however, you have some tables you need to convert or want them to check your work for corrections, then the add-on menu might be for you.

They seem to understand that. While they've tried to make their packages as user-friendly as possibly they might not be perfect for everyone.

Linked to a Random House subsidiary (Random House Ventures) as a strategic partner, Xlibris has been a force in the publishing world for several years now. This partnership though has been a source of confusion for many authors. This arrangement is considered an investment by Random House and does not mean they will automatically consider you. Authors still have to earn the respect of their peers and the sales figures to prove they are worthy of a contract.

Contact Information:
www.xlibris.com
(888) 795-4274

Xlibris		Comments
Package Price	Basic service begins at $500 and goes up to $1600	
Distribution	Ingram	
Retail Book Price	Paperbacks $16 Hardbacks $25	Hardback option is available only through Professional and Premium service
Rights	Stay with the author	
Royalty	10% if purchased through a bookstore, 25% purchased directly from Xlibris.	
Author Discounts	40%	
Time from Manuscript to Book	Approximately two to three months	
Page min/max	100 page min 750 page max	
Approval Process	None	
Hard/softcover	Both	
Royalties Paid	Paid quarterly	
24/7 Sales Tracker	Yes	
Listing with *Books in Print*	Yes	
Cancellation	Either party can cancel this agreement at any time	

Something to Think About

The following books were self-published:

Invisible Life by E. Lynn Harris

The Adventures of Huckleberry Finn by Mark Twain

What Color is Your Parachute? by Richard Bolles

One Minute Manager by Ken Blanchard & Spencer Johnson

The Christmas Box by Rick Evans

In Search of Excellence by Tom Peters

The Celestine Prophecy by James Redfield

Life's Little Instruction Book by H. Jackson Brown

Woman Thou Art Loosed by T.D. Jakes

Brothers Lust and Love by William July II

Emily, The Yellow Rose by Anita Richmond Bunkley

Will the Real Women...Please Stand Up! by Ella Patterson

❧

"Rather than worry about being 'Napstered,' our business should practically be wishing that 20 million young people wanted to trade book files across the Net."

Michael Cader, president of Cader Books

❧

On-Line Publishing Tips

Before we move into the next phase of this book, I want to take a minute to highlight some significant points when selecting an on-line publisher. These points have been excerpted from *Everything You Always Wanted to Know About Print-On-Demand Publishing But Didn't Know Who To Ask* by John Harnish (publisher: Infinity Publishing).

1. Rights: You want to be absolutely certain that you retain all rights to your book. All rights literally means all of the rights—including, but not limited to: foreign, film, audio, hard cover/paperback books, and electronics. Be certain you are only granting revocable permission for the POD publisher to produce and distribute your book as orders are received under a nonexclusive publishing agreement. If the POD publisher you are considering requires you to assign any right to the publisher for a specific period of time be sure to ask what they are going to do in exchange for this time constraint and how will such an assignment benefit you.

2. Copyright: It is in your best interest for you to personally fill out and sign the forms, pay the filing fee and file for your copyright protection with the Library of Congress. By doing it this way you know without a doubt that the copyright is in your name and you receive and retain the certificate of copyright when it is recorded and granted.

3. Fair Usage: Be prepared to provide your POD publisher with copies of permission granting correspondence for any copyright protected material you have included in your book.

4. Cancellation: Look for a hassle free termination clause in the agreement that allows you to withdraw from the publishing arrangement upon written notice (an acknowledged e-mail should be acceptable) to have your book removed from the POD system and their on-line bookstore.

5. Nonexclusive: This means that in addition to your POD publisher you're able to publish your book by other methods of publication—including another POD publisher. However, having two POD books that are the same with the exception of the ISBN—which identifies the publisher—could create confusion when booksellers try to order your book. The nonexclusive provision is most useful when you're making a transition between publishers and perhaps issuing a revised edition. Also, the nonexclusive provision is another way to keep your options open.

6. Control: You must understand completely what aspects of the book you have final say over and what will be decided for you by the POD publisher. Certain book production requirements are fixed can't be changed, such as the minimum and maximum number of pages, the page size, paper weight, and the minimum width of margins. If the POD publisher provides the service of formatting your book for you, be sure you understand if you have any recourse other than accepting what they have done. You must also factor in any surcharges that could apply to formatting your book the way you want it to be. For example, some POD services use a fixed template format that won't allow any deviations, and others are flexible and will work with your formatting as long as you follow their formatting guidelines.

7. Editing and Proofreading: The final editing and proofreading of your book is your responsibility. Your POD publisher is NOT RESPONSIBLE for editing or proofreading your book. In fact most POD publishers will not change a single word in your book without your written instructions to make the change.

8. Graphics: With some POD publishers there could be a surcharge for including illustrations, charts, tables, footnotes, and photographs in your book. Sometimes there's no charge if you have already positioned the graphics on the pages where you want them to appear. If your book is loaded with graphics request a written quote of any additional charges that might apply.

9. Formatting: Most POD publishers have similar formatting guidelines for how you must prepare your book file with regards to page size and margins. Be sure to follow the instructions and call your publisher's representative if you have any questions. An improperly formatted book will create problems during the conversion process.

10. Production Time: This could vary from a few short weeks to many long months of waiting until your book is available for sale. How long often depends on the condition of the book file you've prepared, the work load of the POD's production departments and if they do the conversion work in house or farm it out to a third party. Be sure you have a firm understanding of when you'll receive the first proof copies of your book.

11. Proofing Correction Costs: Usually the setup charges includes making a certain number of changes as part of the proofing process. Additional corrections to the proof copy above the allowed number of changes could incur a surcharge.

12. Corrections After Approval: Remember to find out what the cost is to correct typos after your book has been approved. Some POD publishers will correct a few typos at no charge even after a book has been added to their system. Other POD publishers will charge a flat fee regardless of how minor the changes might be.

13. Revised Editions: There could come a time when you might need to do a major revision or update time critical material in your POD book. Be sure to ask the POD publishers you're considering what their policies and charges are for swapping book files to produce a revised edition of your book. The fee should be considerably less than their initial setup fee because there's usually less work involved. Usually a second edition with significantly new material will require a new ISBN and perhaps another copyright filing. Significantly new material is usually defined as approximately 15 to 20% of the book being reworked with new material.

14. Royalties: Be absolutely certain you completely understand how your earned royalties are calculated. Some POD publishers pay authors a percentage based on the selling price of the book—usually the percentage is higher on retail sales placed directly through the publisher's on-line bookstore and a lower percentage on wholesale orders placed by booksellers. If the net selling price is being used, be sure to understand how much the expenses account for, specifically what the expense items include. Also, ask if expenses are 

likely to increase in the foreseeable future—when an increase of "expenses" happens your royalty percentage stays the same; however, your royalty earnings would decrease because the net selling price debits the expenses.

15. Assignment of Royalties: Some POD publishers will allow the author to assign their royalties to a third party to enable them to benefit from the sale of their book. Such assignments of royalties can be essential if the book is the work product of a group effort. A few will accept a preassignment of royalties to a spouse, offspring, relative, or close friend in the event of the author's death. This will permit the book to continue to be published and royalties paid even after the death of the author.

16. Confidential Information: Be sure you have an understanding of the privacy policies of the POD publishers you are considering. Authors need assurances that if they publish under a pseudonym their true identity will be kept private.

17. Returns: Most POD publishers will not accept books being returned by booksellers. One of the many advantages of POD publishing is that books are only produced in the quantities needed to fill orders. If your POD publisher is factoring "returns" into the book selling and distribution equation be sure you understand what's involved. Usually royalties are never paid on books as long as they are subject to being returned to the publisher for full credit. If your POD publisher accepts returns ask who bears the expense of producing these unsold books and how long is the time period that booksellers have to return them. Frequently when books are returned they are so damaged from being handled that they can't be used to fill another order. You need to determine if entering into an agreement with a POD publisher that accepts returns is really worth the uncertainty of knowing what has actually been sold and what hasn't been sold.

18. Author Book Purchases: Some POD publishers will sell the author's book to the author at a special discount—with some publishers the author's discount of approximately 20%

isn't as good as the standard 40% wholesale discount extended to booksellers. A few POD publishers pay royalties on all purchases of the author's book—even when the author buys their own books at the wholesale price. Check on who pays the shipping charges when an author orders 20 or more copies of their book.

19. Order Taking: Make sure the POD publisher you select is equipped to receive orders for your book 24/7 from customers calling in on a toll free number to a secure automatic order receiving device (this is like a fancy voice mail system that's programmed to receive the information a customer leaves to order a book). In addition to the secure automated order taking system, customers need to be able to fax in an order and also be able to phone in on a toll free number to talk with a real live person during normal business hours. Customers need to be able to pay for book purchases with popular charge cards and checks—even electronic checks. This is important to you because you want a hassle free process for customers ordering your book.

20. Order Delivery Time: Most POD publishers will ship all book orders within 24 to 48 hours. Be sure to confirm what the usual time frame will be to process and fill an order for your book. Nothing will turn a customer off more than having to wait weeks to receive a POD book that they rightfully expected to arrive at their door in only a few days after they've place the order. Prompt order processing and accurate fulfillment are essential for keeping customers happy, building repeat business and to produce those important referrals of more folks interested in ordering your book.

21. Ingram/Lightning Source: Some publishers include the cost of adding your book into the Ingram distribution system as part of the setup fee, others charge a separate fee for Ingram distribution and offer it as an optional service. Lightning Source, a large commercial POD printer located in the Ingram warehouse complex in LaVerne, TN, is a wholly owned subsidiary of Ingram and prints all POD books that are distributed by Ingram. Lightning Source charges publishers a setup fee to add books into their POD system. They also charge an annual maintenance fee that POD publishers with books in the Ingram/Lightning Source distribution system must pay to maintain their books to fulfill all orders for POD books from Ingram. If your book is being sold through Ingram be sure you have an understanding of what kind of arrangement is in place between your POD publisher and Ingram/Lightning Source. Lightning Source pays POD publishers a percentage of all their titles produced and sold on a 90 day cycle. This kind of payment schedule could delay your publisher dispersing royalty payments on sales made to bookstores through Ingram. The reason for the delay is most likely because of Ingram's imposed book return policy. There's a very good chance that all or part of the annual maintenance charges from Lightning Source and Ingram to their publishers will be passed on to their authors with POD books in the Lightning Source/Ingram distribution system.

22. Annual Maintenance and Listing Fees: Some POD publishers are charging annual fees to maintain your book in their POD system or to keep your book listed in their on-line bookstore—this is often in addition to the fees imposed by distributors. You are obligated to pay these imposed ongoing costs even if you haven't sold enough books to cover the charge. Unfortunately not selling books in sufficient amounts to cover these continuing costs is a potential risk. Failure to pay will result in having your book (that you thought would never go out of print) pulled from their POD inventory unless you come up with the money to maintain its presence on the publisher's on-line bookstore. If Lightning Source is involved your book will be purged from their system and from Ingram distribution as well for nonpayment of their fees. What these fees provide for the POD publishers is a way to produce an ongoing cash flow even if your book doesn't sell—or only sells a few copies each month. They're hedging their bet to generate income from your book regardless of what you do or don't do to promote your book. Make it a point to ask if you'll be expected to pay these fees that are usually required to be paid in advance.

23. Thresholds: A few POD publishers are implementing the concept of threshold achievements for authors. When an author's book has sold a certain number of copies then those accumulated sales will clearly demonstrate the marketability of the book. Because of the encouraging book orders several things are able to happen to further benefit the author. The percentage of their royalty increases, the author qualifies to participate in co-op advertising sponsored in part by the publisher, and increased efforts are made to gain more exposure for the book.

24. Guaranteed Delivery: When you have to fly somewhere to do a public speaking engagement with an opportunity to sell your book you need to be sure you have books to sell. These days, you don't need the additional hassle of trying to pack books in your luggage. Find out if your POD publisher will ship your books directly to the hotel and guarantee the delivery to arrive before you check in. A few publishers will pay normal ground shipping charges when you order 20 or more books. Check with your POD publisher to find out the lead time needed for your books to be delivered when needed to a third party location.

25. Transitional Services: Even high speed digital presses can reach a point when demand for a book exceeds the production capabilities of the POD equipment. When keeping up with an increasing flow of orders ceases to be cost effective you need a POD publisher with the means of arranging a print run on an offset press. You might want to amend your agreement to allow your POD publisher to make these arrangements on your behalf and so can continue to publish under the house name of your POD publisher, or give you assistance to exercise your option to make your own preparations for a commercial print run. It could also happen that a traditional publisher will make you an offer. You need a POD publisher able to work with you and help you through this transitional period by keeping your book available until your traditionally published book is released.

26. Redundant Backups: Paramount to the effective operations of every POD publisher are the author's book files that are used by the POD system to produce books. These vital files are their inventory. Without these files there's nothing to sell. Redundant backup files are constantly being created to insure their ability to maintain a virtually interruption free operation. In our instant gratification seeking society unforeseen delays can be totally devastating to a publisher's ability to continue to do business.

27. Policy Changes: Be sure to ask about how and when authors will be notified about future policy changes that could impact your book and the agreement you have entered into with the POD publisher. Some changes that provide additional benefits to authors are made retroactively so both their current and new authors can benefit from the newly implemented policies. This can be good or bad depending on what's involved. Watch out if your POD publisher tries to suddenly make a new charge for services retroactive and they assess you with a fee for previous services rendered. Don't pay it—instead take a close look at your publishing agreement and give serious consideration to exercising your right to terminate your relationship with them at once.

4

What About An Agent?

If you're wondering about the agent-factor in all of this, consider this. According to a recent polling of literary agents, 40% of them say they won't take an unknown author for the same reason publishers are leery of publishing them. And since you don't need an agent to approach these types of publishers, why bother with them? You can, of course, try to garner attention from your novel once you have a proven track record. You could also use your track record to try to publish traditionally in the future. The choice is yours. Keep in mind that every decision you make regarding your book is setting the stage for future novels and for your reputation as an author. Traditional publishers will consider reprinting books that have a good track record. Take a look at *The Bridges of Madison County* as an example. This book was published initially by a smaller house, then, when it seemed it would take off, a larger company stepped in. The rest is history.

So, while an agent seems ideal, you don't need one for these types of publishers nor should you waste your time (and theirs) pursuing one. Of course, given the expansion of this industry, literary agents may be changing their business models. For the time being though, an agent is there to garner you attention from a traditional publisher. If your book is doing well, you might think about submitting it to an agent for their consideration. If it's selling well in the self-publishing arena, they might be interested in representing you. After all, there's nothing quite like a sure thing.

❧

Something to think about:

In a survey of 80 top literary agents, it was discovered that they typically reject 98% of what they receive. The rejection rate is far higher for fiction than nonfiction.

5

Cultivating Your Relationship With Amazon.com

I encourage you to make the most of your relationship with Amazon. Next to your local bookstore, they should be your new best friend. When I initially got my book onto their site, I contacted their Author Services Department (book-dept@amazon.com). They directed me to a section of their site where I could add my own book description (very important) and conduct an on-line author interview. All of these things lend to additional exposure for your book and assist in book sales. Once that was done, I contacted them again to find out where I could send my book for review. We'll discuss more on reviews later in this book, but suffice to say that a review at Amazon is worth its weight in gold. Also, if you've got the time, head on over to: http://www.amazon.com/exec/obidos/subst/partners/publishers/publishers.html/103-0158948-3135821. This link will take you directly into their publisher pages. From there you can upload all sorts of content adding it directly to their site. The publisher page will allow you to add you table of contents, a sample chapter, reviews, a blurb about yourself, and several other pieces of pertinent information that will help encourage people to buy your book.

A couple of numbers to remember: Author Services can be reached at the E-mail address above or via telephone at (206) 266-2952. Try E-mailing them first though because they respond very quickly that way.

If you notice anything at all that you need to correct in your book description you can reach the book corrections department at book-typos@amazon.com. Remember to always include your book title and ISBN number with all correspondence. They keep over four million titles in their inventory so you can imagine how tough it is to find your book on the title alone.

Tip: If you need to supply your own cover art to Amazon be forewarned that sending it via E-mail or disk can take weeks to appear. If you FTP it, the art will go up in 24 hours.

The Secrets To Their Ranking System

If you've ever been on the Amazon site, you'll notice that they've got something called an Amazon Sales Rank. When I first got published, I checked this sales rank number every few hours. Okay, okay, I checked it much more than that. It was a lot like when I bought my first stock and I was on-line checking it every ten minutes. Yet, at the same time, it's much more personal than checking stock because everything you do seems to affect this number. There were days when it soared into the 700 range and other days when it plummeted to the mid-500,000 range. Yes, I was put on suicide watch during that time.

The truth is, that while many have tried to crack this secret code, few have been successful. It does go up and down based on sales (some of it might also be driven by the number of hits on their site) but how many one needs to sell, to garner that elusive #1 spot is not known. Any book ranked at 10,000 or less gets an hourly update, rankings of 100,000 or so are based on sales in the past thirty days and the rest are based on sales at Amazon since the company's inception. Barnes and Noble has a much more simplified version of this numbering system. Their rankings are based on their brick and mortar stores as well as on-line sales over the past six months.

A much more industry-wide accepted ranking is that of USA Today or the New York Times (although the accuracy of these lists are debatable at times). Since those types of lists aren't always available to the on-line published author, we have to take what we can get. If you've watched a book's sales ranking for any amount of time you'll notice that they can be pretty erratic. These numbers can jump by the thousands each day. It's both intriguing and frustrating. Exactly how many books it takes to move that magical number is still a mystery, but I enjoy watching it nonetheless.

6

Stuff To Do Before It's A Book

Taking Care Of Business

Well, you're a business now. Or, at least if you aren't, you should be. Here are a couple of things to consider taking care of before you begin the process of publishing.

⚹ Get your Business License

You may want to just go under your own name, or you may want to file a fictitious business name or DBA ("doing business as"). Contact your local city offices to find out what's needed for each. Usually when filing a DBA, you have to go down and search the directory to make sure that the snazzy name you've picked for your company hasn't been picked up by someone else. Once you've established that no one else has the name, you can file for it. After which, you'll need to run an ad in a local paper. But don't worry about trying to find a paper to place that ad. Literally seven minutes after you walk out of the building, advertisements start to appear in your mailbox telling you where the best deals are for running a fictitious business name ad.

❧ Get a PO Box

Trust me on this one. Do not, under any circumstances, give out your home address. Someday when you've written a book that pushes the envelope and you have every lunatic on your doorstep you'll thank me. You would not believe some of the stories I've heard over the years. Keep your peace of mind; spend the forty bucks and get a box. You'll sleep better knowing that no matter how famous you get, no one will be sneaking up to your house at night to dig through your trash.

❧ Open a Checking Account

Commercial accounts are expensive. I recommend opening a personal account, especially, if you're not using a fictitious business name. As long as it's separate from your household account you should be fine. But, since I'm am a long way off from being the queen of accounting, you might want to double check this.

❧ Creating Your Identity Package

Getting an identity package is an essential part of your business. One of the reasons that I don't use a fictitious name for my company is that all my identity materials will tend to reflect a recent book release. For example when *The Cliffhanger* came out, I had stationery, postcards, business cards and bookmarks all made up with the same logo and cover photo. Consistency is key here. Business names when you're trying to push your book can sometimes confuse people, especially if your book is fiction. If you're running a candy shop and your book is on the health benefits of gummy bears that might be a different story. Take a long hard look at what you are presenting to the world and how it will be perceived. Run your identity package by a few friends or business associates, if you can.

❧ Telephone

Do you have a lot of people using one phone? If so, you might want to think about getting a separate line for your business. Even if you don't having others sharing your phone, you still might want to consider it. Since you have a license to operate, you can write it off anyway. It's also good so that you're not answering your business phone at all hours either. If you're dealing with a lot of people on a different coast, there's a three hour time differential. This might cause you to get calls at say…3 a.m. Yeah, that's what I thought. As much as I want to get that call from the *New York Times* telling me they want to run my story, I'd rather be coherent when I speak with them.

❧ Answering Machine

Have you called yourself lately? Maybe you should try to. What you hear when you're not there to answer is what that all important media contact will hear as well. Keep it professional and keep it brief, and plug whatever you have going on at the moment. Do it tactfully, or people will get sick of waiting through your five minute message and hang up.

❧ Uncle Sam

As you begin your journey to being a business owner, check with the IRS to see what you can write off and what you can't. Are you using a separate room for your office? If so, you might be able to deduct a portion of it on your taxes. If you're having to buy a lot of new office equipment, check first to see if you should take the deduction all at once or if you should depreciate it. That's all I'm going to say about that because my tax forms may as well be written in Mandarin Chinese for all I know. Every year I hand a stack of well-worn receipts over to my tax guy and pray.

Don't Forget!

Before you send your book to your publisher of choice,
have a photo of yourself taken. You'll definitely need a
black and white photo and maybe a color photo as well. Get
creative with these.

7

Don't Let Someone
Steal Your Stuff

Copyright, copyright, copyright. That's what I tell people who attend my seminars. It's vitally important to protect your writing
and your rights. Sending a copy of it to yourself will not cover you
in a court of law. This came directly from an attorney I consulted
on the issue. You've got to package it and send it to the US Copyright Office with the proper form and a
thirty dollar copyright fee.

You can obtain the copyright
form one of two ways. First, you
can download it from their web site
at www.loc.gov/copyright/forms/.
Click on FormTX and FormTX instructions. This will launch your Acrobat Reader and *voila!*, you'll have
everything you need to register your
manuscript. If you don't want to download these forms off of the
Internet, you can also obtain them by writing:

Registrar of Copyrights
Library of Congress
Washington, DC 20559

Request three copies of the FormTX as well as a set of instructions. They did not indicate that you needed to include a self-addressed stamped envelope, but it probably wouldn't hurt.

Now, for shipping and storing they recommend binding your manuscript, whether it's spiral or some other type of binding. Don't paperclip or staple your stuff. They say it stores poorly this way and comes apart more easily. Believe it or not, they have actually gotten works small enough to paper clip.

Once you send your manuscript to them, it will take approximately three to four months to get back a form stating that your manuscript is officially protected. It took six months for me one time; it just depends how busy they are.

Similar to a patent, a copyright will protect your written works. They are less expensive and easier to obtain than a patent and will cover photographs, drawings, text, maps and anything else in your book except for the title. The term of the copyright is the author's life plus fifty years. Keep in mind that your ownership of this is now an important part of your estate, so don't forget to mention your copyrighted material in your will.

Trademarking

Copyrighting your book does not protect the title. That's where a little thing called trademarking comes in. If you have a book title you're thinking of merchandising or spinning off into a collection of products or services, then trademarking might be for you. Before you go through the trouble of trademarking your title. You'll want to do a thorough search of the name first. Make sure someone else doesn't have it before you start the trademarking process. The *Internet Movie Database* is a good place to start. You can search their database by going to http://us.imdb.com/search. When you're done searching movie tiles, go over to Amazon.com and search their database for book titles as well. If after searching both of those databases it still looks like your title is free and clear then go over to Lyrics World at www.lyricsworld.com and search there as well. If your title hasn't been used it's time to visit the US Patent and Trademarking site at www.uspto.gov and begin your trademarking process. Keep in mind that if this process seems a bit overwhelming you can always retain a trademarking attorney to handle this for you.

Although you can't copyright your book title, you can establish a trademark. Check out the following site to learn more about obtaining a trademark for your title: www.uspto.gov/web/offices/tac/doc/basic/.

Sites

Publaw.com is a great site to explore the issues of copyrighting and fair use.

Nolopress.com is another great legal site. They offer hundreds of books on just about any law-related topic you can imagine. They also have a great section on copyright law.

8

Can You Tell A Book By Its Cover?

Yes, you most certainly can. One of your biggest sales tools is your book cover. Did you know that if someone sees your book on the shelf, you have less than thirty seconds to sell it? The cover of your book is extremely important. Often, people are attracted to your book by its stunning colors or catchy title. Remember that your book cover will not only be on your book, but it will more than likely grace most or all of your marketing materials as well. The main color will probably be a general theme or set the tone for your marketing package. You want to stay consistent and look professional. One way of achieving this is through a well thought out cover and coordinated marketing materials.

A great piece of advice that someone once gave me was to peruse the merchandise in a bookstore. Spend an afternoon, or whatever you can, looking over books similar to yours. Decide what works for them and what does not. Then, go home and design a cover that fits your audience. While most on-line publishers will do this work for you, you want to enter into this part of the process with a full understanding of what you want and what your final product should look like. If it starts to get too complicated, consider hiring a graphic designer to do this work for you. My graphic designer has done several marketing pieces for me as well as assisting me with several cover designs. She offered the following tips for front cover, back cover and spine:

Front cover

- Contrast is key. Draw attention to your book by using a lighter background with darker color type or vice versa. Also, avoid choosing a color for your title that merges into the background.
- Make sure that the title and subtitle are in different fonts to draw a distinction between the two.
- Don't use all caps; it can give a very angry impression. Instead, use both upper and lower-case letters.
- As a rule of thumb, the title should be visible from about 12 feet away, which means letters no smaller than 24 pt (1/3 inch) and preferably 36 pt (½ inch).

Back cover

- The back cover should list the benefits of the book. Promise health, wealth, entertainment or a better life. Make it catchy and thought provoking. Again, visiting a bookstore will help you decide what draws you to a book and what's a real turn off.
- If you're fortunate enough to have garnered pre-production blurbs or endorsements from reviewers or specialists in your topic, don't overuse them. I know you're thrilled to have so many people praising your book, but don't fill your back cover with every single one you've ever gotten. Use the most significant one on the cover,

put one or two on the back and if you have more, use the first few pages of your book.

- The blurb about yourself should be no more than three sentences. I know, I know, you have so much to say, so much talent and so many other books waiting in the wings. But try to limit this; trust me, they may love your book, but they really don't want to hear all about you.

Spine

- Make sure that your name and the title of the book are prominent and easy to read.
- Don't use a complicated font. Keep it simple and easy to read.

❧

Did you know?

If you thought the front cover received an unfair thirty-second judgment call, the back cover only receives fifteen seconds.

9

The Name Game

Titling your book can be a tricky thing; ask anyone who has spent any time at all trying to play the name game. It can be perplexing and it will often determine the future of your book. "Keywords aren't just for the Web," says Mary Westheimer, CEO of BookZone.com, the Net's largest publishing community. "Including keywords in your title makes it easy for anyone to ascertain that you are indeed covering a particular subject, and starting your title with a keyword can be the best of all."

A good title should draw attention away from all the other books sitting on the shelf around it. It should be enticing and thought provoking and anything but dull. You need to target your audience with this title. Ask yourself who's going to be buying your book and what's their age group? Joan Stewart, The Publicity Hound (www.publicityhound.com), gave me the following tips for coming up with a killer title:

During your visit to the bookstore, scan the cover of magazines and compile a list of clever titles that capture your attention. Even if the titles have nothing to do with your book, sometimes you can substitute a word or two to come up with a title that's a perfect fit for your topic.

Name three of the biggest problems your book helps readers solve. You've just come up with three more possible titles or chapter headings.

Write them down and let them ferment, then experiment with an unusual play on words.

Brainstorm ideas with your friends. Give them three possible titles and ask them to choose their favorite.

Scan titles and chapter headings in other books. Borrow a word here, a clever turn of phrase there. Keep massaging the title until you come up with something you like and most importantly, something that others like.

Some of the most successful titles are those that answer the reader's question: "What's in it for me?" or "Why should I care?" People want books that will inspire, educate, calm, enlighten, humor and entertain. Choose a title that answers those two questions and you're well on your way.

Changed book titles

Tomorrow is Another Day… *Gone With the Wind*
Blossom & the Flower… *Peyton Place*
Something that Happened… *Of Mice and Men*
John Thomas & Lady Jane… *Lady Chatterly's Lover*

If you're writing an advice book, the title can explain outcomes and timetable for achieving them. Example: *25 Things You Can Do This Week To Save Thousands Next Year!*

Did you know?

Bookstore databases typically only store the first 30 characters of a book title. So, if you have a longer-than-thirty-character name, guess what? It gets cut off. That's why a lot of publishers will reverse the name of a book, especially if it's nonfiction so the subject matter comes first. For example *Get Published Today!* was originally: *An Author's Guide to On-Line Publishing*. Had I left it with the original title it would have left a lot of people wondering *An Author's Guide...* to what?

10

Cover Images

If you're thinking of getting a cover photo for your book, there are a number of on-line stock photo shops you can peruse. When deciding on a cover photo for *The Cliffhanger*, I must have waded through 2,500 photos before I found exactly the right one. That's how significant this is. Photos should typically be about 300 dpi for cover images. This is what most on-line publishers will accept, but check with them first as their requirements may have changed. When using a cover image, I recommend going through a stock photo company unless you have a picture you want to use and the necessary permissions to put it on the cover of your book. Don't shortchange yourself on this. Assume that your book is going to be a national bestseller, you don't want to take any chances with copyright infringements here. People will see the picture and often recognize it so get your permissions in writing.

Two stock photo companies I've used are:

- www.gettyimages.com
- www.corbis.com

❧ Something to consider

Did you know that, whether for themselves or someone else, women buy the majority of books on the market? Designing a cover that grabs the attention of a woman is probably not a bad idea.

11

What's An ISBN?

The ISBN (International Standard Book Number) system
uniquely identifies all books published worldwide. All parts of
the book trade use these identification numbers for inventory
control, ordering and accounting. About a million ISBNs are assigned each year for English-language publications alone.

An ISBN is a unique and unchangeable number, identifying
one title published by one publisher. The first six digits identify the
publisher and are publisher specific. If you publish through one
company, then, later switch your book to another your ISBN
number will change. The final digit is a mathematical check digit.
Because all publishers' contact information is kept current at
common reference sources, such as R.R. Bowker's *Books-In-
Print* catalog and database, bookstores and librarians worldwide
can determine quickly where to purchase a copy. The ISBN identifies a "publisher," rather than the author, since people in the
book trade expect to order from the publisher. Although, techni-
cally you are self-publishing, most often it is the publisher who
handles distribution, and consequently, all orders are filtered
through them.

Marketing,
Not For The Faint Of Heart

12

Becoming A Marketing Guru

So who's responsible for promoting your book? Why, you, of course, the author, the one who gave birth to this awesome venture. Now, before you launch head first into marketing consider this for a moment. Over 100,000 titles are published each year in the United States alone. That figures to approximately 300 titles released each day. Over 1.3 million books are in print or currently available. To display all of these books, a bookstore would need five miles of shelf space. When you consider that most bookstores stock 40,000 to 80,000 titles, how in the world are people going to know your book exists?

Because you're going to shout it from the mountain tops. Because you're going to invent and then reinvent the wheel on this. Because although you don't know it yet, you are a marketing guru!

Write the book,
Publish the book,
Sell the book.

Jim Donovan on becoming a literary success.
www.freelancehelp.com

ß

Marketing Tip:

Want to bring your book to the attention of store personnel? Try "planting" your book in the store. That's right. In
other words, reverse shop-lift. Leave it, face out on a shelf
somewhere and let someone buy it. Certainly when the
cashier tries to ring up the sale and the book doesn't appear in inventory, someone will notice.

ß

13

Your Publication Date

When I first began the process of marketing *The Cliffhanger*, I kept running into a term that often confused me. "Publication date." It seemed like this indefinable date was somewhere between writing the thing and getting it published. Upon further research I found that a publication date is decided on by you—usually four months after your book rolls off the presses. This date will usually coincide with your media blitz. Sometimes publishers and authors tie in their publication date to specific anniversaries or dates that might be significant to the book. Generally, publishers bring out books in the fall and in the spring. The more savvy marketing individual realizes that there are in fact, many more dates to choose from. Think of Mother's Day, Valentine's Day, Father's Day, Secretary's Day, Easter, Passover, Fourth of July, Halloween, Thanksgiving and of course, Christmas. When deciding on your publication date, I suggest getting a book called *Celebrate Today*. If you can, tie in your book's publication date to a particular holiday. This book is filled with special dates you know well and some you've never even heard of. You can take a look at their web site at www.celebratetoday.com and even order your copy ($9.95) on-line.

A publication date is also significant when getting your book reviewed. Generally, book reviewers have specific guidelines for accepting books before or after a publication date. Reviewers receive on average of 2500 to 3500 titles per month. And while they won't review everything they receive, more often than not, you must allow ample review time to be considered. Some reviewers don't want a book that's been out for a few months, hence you'll see the term "pre-publication reviews." Then, there are those reviewers who don't care if a book has been out for a while, they are your "post-publication" reviewers (we discuss these terms at length in the "Let's Review" section of this book). According to Jim Cox of the *Midwest Book Review*, they receive an average of 1500 titles per month. "So in addition to the physical appearance of their book, the content of their book, the quality of their publicity release and/or media kit, the very timing of submissions has a great deal to do with how the small press can successfully compete with the large publishers for a reviewer's attention."

14

Who's Your Market?

When I talk to authors about their books, one of the first questions I ask them is: Who's your audience? Most authors will smile proudly and say: "Everyone!" Well, guess what folks? If your audience is "everyone" then your market is not focused and you'll have too much competition. By narrowing your market and knowing your reader, you can hone in on a specific group of people. The fact of the matter is that book marketing should begin while the book is still being written. Why? Because your subject matter, your characters, dialogues, etc. will all reflect your specific reader demographic. For example, if you're writing a novel for the teenage crowd you might want to think about using a setting they can respond to. For most teenagers, it's futuristic. Writing a novel set during the sixties might not entice them to read on. But, if you were writing a book for the baby boomer generation, something set in the sixties might be perfect. The same holds true for nonfiction. Again, you're writing for a specific market. If it's a how-to book, you'll need to know how advanced your reader is. Are they a beginner or have they had some expertise with your topic? The *Idiots Guide* books do well because their market is very specific. You might refute this because their subject matter is so broad. But guess what each of their readers has in common? They're all beginners.

When you're beginning your book outline, it probably wouldn't hurt to take a moment to see what everyone else is doing. Get on Amazon.com, BN.com or any one of the on-line bookstores and see what's out there. Order them or go to your local library. The key here is to find out what's working and what isn't. Know your competition. So what if you're writing something that's already been done. Perhaps you're reinventing the wheel, or, maybe you're looking at the same topic from a different angle. I mean, when I was considering writing this book, I almost gave up when I realized how many books on book marketing there were out there. But, you know what? Mine is different. Yours can be too.

If you've been marketing your book for a while with little or no momentum, think about redefining your reader. I spoke to an associate of mine who is doing this with her book. Initially, her audience seemed obvious but as she began marketing she realized it was in fact an entirely different age group. Sometimes that happens. You'll be marketing your book to one particular group when you realize they're not your target at all. Sometimes this can't be avoided, sometimes book marketing isn't the exact science we'd like it to be. Still, asking yourself a few specific questions can probably help save you valuable marketing dollars and even more valuable time.

Here are some questions to help you better define your audience:

- How old is my reader?

- Is my reader male or female?
- Where does my reader live?
- How educated is my reader?
- What makes my reader happy?
- What saddens my reader?
- What are their fears?
- What are their aspirations?
- What do they need most in their life?
- What does your reader do for a living?
- Is my reader married, single, or divorced?
- Is my reader a parent?
- What does my reader do in his or her spare time?
- What types of books does my reader already read?

By knowing some or all of the above, you'll really be able to get a handle on who you're marketing to. As you dig into the life of your reader all sorts of things will begin to emerge. For example possible associations they belong to and magazines and books they read. This will not only tell you how to market effectively, but how also allow you to create a book that feels as though it was written just for your reader. A book that when finished, will excite and enlighten them and make them want to pass it on. Think about this for a second. How many times have you finished a book and said: "Well, the first part was good, but the last three chapters were kind of a waste of my time." Making your reader feel good, informed or entertained from start to finish will not only leave you with a happy reader but a walking, talking advertisement for your book and a fan for all of your future works.

When you know who your market is, you can begin a more directed campaign. Also, you can begin to join some on-line newsgroups related to your market, organizations or other areas that can draw attention to your book. Also, by joining groups related to your book, you will begin to learn about other areas for potential sales. For example, if your book is senior citizen related, you can begin to explore magazines, newsletters and communities directed at seniors. If your book is related to children of divorced parents, you have a whole different area to pursue. Try hooking up with local organizations such as PWP (Parents without Partners). Offer to do a talk at one of their meetings. When you join on-line newsgroups; offer advice; be helpful. Try to find any and all trade magazines related to your topic. If you are writing a book about gardening, I know for a fact that there are at least fifty gardening magazines and newsletters in my area alone to get you started. If your book is a mystery, try joining some mystery groups and on-line chats. Check out www.about.com and head to their reading room section. You'll find a myriad of selections from which you can choose.

Marketing Tip:

Did you know that the over 40 group of women is soon to be the largest and the wealthiest demographic in the country? If you're not currently targeting this group of women, you might want to consider doing so.

"You've already heard it a million times…know your audience. As I wrote Beyond the Blues—Treating Depression One Day at a Time, *I wrote each day of this daily meditation book with the vision of a person who is in desperate need of some encouragement, comfort and support. I approach marketing and promotion with the same vision…the vision of getting this book in the hands of some lost soul who may be in desperate need of some experience, strength, and hope!"*

Edward F. Haas, http://www.treatingdepression.com/

&

15

Know Your Category

*K*nowing what category your book is in will go a long way to helping you to further determine your audience. The Book Industry Systems Advisory Committee has developed over 2,000 subjects and subject codes used to describe the contents of a specific title. From those 2,000 different subject categories, 46 major categories have emerged. Knowing what these are will help you determine where your book fits into the grand scheme of things and how bookstores will shelve your book, should they decide to carry it.

- Antiques/Collectibles
- Architecture
- Biography/Autobiography/Letters
- Business/Economics/Finance
- Computer Technology & Software
- Cookbooks & Cookery
- Crafts & Hobbies
- Current Affairs
- Drama
- Education & Teaching
- Family/Child Care/Relationships

- Fiction/Literature
- Foreign Language Instruction & Reference
- Games
- Gardening & Horticulture
- Health & Fitness
- History
- Home Improvement & Construction
- Humor
- Language Arts
- Law
- Literary Criticism & Essays
- Mathematics
- Medical/Nursing/Home Care
- Music
- Nature & Natural History
- Occultism/Parapsychology
- Performing Arts
- Pets & Pet Care
- Philosophy, Photography
- Poetry
- Political Science & Government
- Psychology/Psychiatry
- Reference
- Religion/Bibles
- Science
- Self-Actualization/Self-Help
- Social Sciences
- Sports & Recreation
- Study Aids
- Technology & Industrial Arts
- Transportation
- Travel & Travel Guides
- True Crime*

---

*Thanks to BookZonePro (www.bookzonepro) for this information

If your title does not fit into any of these categories, contact:

R.R.. Bowker Data Collection Center
P.O. Box 6000-0103
Oldsmar FL 34677-0103
(800) 521-8110 (Reed Reference)
E-mail: info@reedref.com

They might be able to guide you to your correct category choice.

16

Media Kits

A lot has been said about these handy things, but one idea reigns supreme. They must be creative and they must look professional. Don't waste an editor or producer's time with sending out a media kit packed full of stuff no one will be interested in. There are a few important things every kit should include:

- Cover Letter
- Author Bio
- Fact sheet with the following information on it: Book Title, Author, Publisher, ISBN, Price, Pub Date, Type of Book i.e. Hard Cover or Trade Paper
- News Release
- Newspaper Clippings
- Newsletter

The final item is something I put together in my media kit, and I have to say, I got rave reviews on it. A newsletter is a simple, preferably colorful, way to highlight all the activity surrounding your book release. This serves two purposes. First of all, it alleviates a busy reporter having to sift through your entire media kit (which they probably won't, unless your name is Dean Koontz), and it also spotlights activity in a one page, (or double sided if it's two pages—you lucky dog) colorful, easy-to-read newsletter. And, by all means, go to two pages if it becomes too crowded. You don't want to make it tough to read. You want it to be easy to scan. I usually include a column on author appearances, a list where the book is available and any places where it's gotten reviewed. If the review is bad, just say: "Reviewed by XXX" (replace the XXX with the publication name or reviewer).

Another good thing to include in your media kit is a list of about ten to twelve questions about you and your book. These could possibly turn out to be your interview questions so keep them interesting and make sure you have some great answers lined up. A tip sheet is another good thing to think about adding to your kit. A tip sheet is a list of ten things excerpted from your book. For example, for *Get Published!* I might want to put a list of ten things to look for in a good on-line publisher, or a list of must-do marketing tactics. This tip sheet will often vary depending on the type of story you are pitching and what angle you are taking. The media loves tip sheets. That way they can reprint your "tips" as a sidebar to your story.

A media kit can also be as simple as a CD with a presentation in PowerPoint. I don't know how open the media is to this form of press kit just yet since the concept is fairly new, but I do know that if you can save them time and give them a spiffy story idea, you've got it made.

One final note on press kits: several books that I read stated that media folders should be black. I say: "Why?" It's depressing and it's what everyone else is doing. When I sent my media kit and review copy to Charles McStravick, of *Readers & Writers Magazine*, he mentioned to me that one of the reasons he was more inclined to look at my package, rather than the other twenty he received that day, was because mine was the only one that wasn't black. It stood out. Your media kit should do the same.

17

Press Release Savvy

*I*t's often stated that press releases should only be used for major events. I disagree with this statement. Take a look at some major companies. Go into their Investor Relations section or Company Information. There you will usually find a lot of press releases on anything and everything the company has to announce. They can cover job promotions, improved products or even personnel changes. When planning your marketing strategy, I say, "less is less." Go for the big time. If you can get your name in front of someone at least seven times over the next eighteen months then you've, at the very least, caught their attention. That's what it takes according to leaders in the marketing and promotions industry. So think about what you want to announce. First and foremost, will be this wonderful book you just wrote. Then, every time some event occurs surrounding this release, write something about it. Tell the world! Of course, don't overdo it, or people will become wise to you and think you're always crying wolf. But when an event merits mentioning, by all means, mention it. Got a book signing? Send a press release. Did you sell your 10,000th book? By all means, send a press release.

Think about it this way; conversations evaporate. Begin seeing your book as a conversation. You have to manage it, keep it going, and keep people talking. That's your objective (that, and selling a million books, but we'll get to that later). It is up to you to educate the media on you and your book. This gives you name recognition, visibility and credibility. Manage this conversation, and manage it right. You'll find people will start talking about your book. Now, if you think that sending one press release will generate enough conversation to get people interested, think again. Unless you have some major, unbelievable hook, it will probably take hundreds of releases to create that clamored-after "buzz" we always hear everyone talk about. But keep it up. A hundred releases really isn't that many, and you'll be amazed how quickly you blow through your ream of paper when announcement time comes around.

Press release template:

FOR IMMEDIATE RELEASE
CONTACT:
Contact person
Company Name
Telephone number
Fax number
E-mail addressPhoto of your book
Web site address

photo of your book

Headline
(really draw their attention with this one)

Title of your book in **BIG BOLD LETTERS**
Author name (optional)

San Diego, California, November 2, 2002—Opening paragraph. This paragraph should contain the most important elements: who, what, when, where and why. Make them want to continue reading.

Body: This area should include information relevant to your book. Don't ramble on here. Keep it brief, stress the positive or the angle.

Closing paragraph should include a short summation of your book info, a short author bio or company history, and how they can obtain their free review copy.

The following information should be at the very bottom of your press release:

Title of your book	Author:
Trade Paperback	ISBN:
Publication Date:	Pages (number of pages)
Price:	Size: (book size)

Available from: Your publisher
To order call: publisher's order number

At the very bottom of your release should be the words (centered)-- 30-- or ###. This tells the media that the release is complete and that there are no more pages.

###

What if my press release goes longer than one page?

Ideally, it's best to keep your press release to one page, but if you MUST go to a second page this is how to do a page break:

-more-

(top of second page)
Headline—abbreviated (page 2)

Remainder of text

Then close with the end comment as discussed above and specific book information below that. Do not repeat this book information on both pages as it becomes confusing, and too much of it will detract from your release.

If you want to take a look at some more examples of press releases head on over to *BookFlash* at www.bookflash.com .

Did you know?

Pretend for a moment that you're a busy editor. Phones are ringing off the hook, stories are breaking and someone has just handed you a press release. You've only got time to read the first three lines of this release before you decide whether to keep it or have it hit the circular file.

❧

❧ **Components of a Successful Press Release:**

- It must be newsworthy.
- Remember, even though I've outlined some specific guidelines for you, press releases aren't a one-size fits all kind of a thing. Tailor them to your media, your book and your target audience.

- Know your audience. Who will be reading your press release?
- Make it simple. Keep it short and write your release in such a way that a busy reporter could easily reuse it for their story.
- Remember the first three-line rule. Your first ten words must be effective.
- Don't misquote; deal with facts and make sure they are accurate.
- Make sure your press release has substance to it and don't pitch needlessly. Eventually the media will be on to you and you'll get ignored.
- Do you have some pithy quotes or reviews you can add? Then by all means include them. Reporters love quotes.
- Provide all of your contact information: address, phone, fax, E-mail, and web site.
- Make sure your press release is in the proper format.
- If you're sending your press release via E-mail, copy and paste it into the body of the text. Don't send it as an attachment. Unless they've specifically asked you to do this. It WILL get deleted.
- If you can send a press release with a customized cover letter, all the better. Offer a story suggestion in your letter, or play on a story they've recently featured and suggest a follow-up.

Here are some great places to post your press release for free:

- www.ebookbroadcast.com
- www.pressbox.co.uk
- www.prweb.com
- www.skali.com
- www.webharbor.com

Once your press release is done, post it to one of these sites and watch your exposure soar.

18

Expert Sheets

One day, I was on a conference call with a morning show producer who said that she wished she had a list of available experts in every imaginable category. That way, when she needed an expert, she could very easily find one. I realized that most producers probably shared her sentiment. That led me to wonder how I could make sure to keep my "expert" clients in the forefront when a related news story broke. The result of this was what I call the Expert Sheet. An Expert Sheet is a simple release stating who the expert is and why. Credentials are important here so make sure and include those as well. Then, I keep them on file and whenever I see something in the news that relates to any one of my clients I quickly fax them over. Expert sheets don't have to be used solely for breaking news; they can also be used to stay in the forefront of a any particular genre you are an expert in. For example, let's say your topic is child care. You might want to send your expert sheet to all parenting related magazines on a monthly basis. That way, if they have a story in the queue they might consider contacting you.

A sample Expert Sheet follows on the next page. Keep in mind that an expert sheet should include two things: the tie-in and the expert's credentials. The media is very credential heavy. They want to know whoever is being interviewed had the schooling or background to substantiate an interview.

Expert Sheet

The following expert is available for comment
Contact: (858) 560-0121

AS THE COUNTRY CONTINUES TO GRIEVE:

EXPERT TO COMMENT ON LOSS AND GRIEVING DURING THE HOLIDAY SEASON

The country continues to grieve as the holiday season approaches

Expert Susan Gilbert knows first hand what it's like to lose someone during the holiday season. Several years ago Susan lost her husband and her mother shortly thereafter. At twenty-five, she was forced to face the holidays alone. "It's not just the loss of those precious lives, but the destruction of two landmarks and the loss of our nation's security. Many people aren't ready for the holiday season and are finding little reason to be joyful this year." Says Gilbert.

Susan Gilbert's background

Susan Gilbert has become an expert on grieving and has spoken to many organizations around the country. She has counseled both adults and children. Her simple message of "taking one step" has been hailed as an extremely "powerful and effective" form of therapy. She began a grassroots campaign from her book called "The Land of I Can", and is now spreading the message of "I Can!" around the country in a time when people often feel "they can't." Her books have been sent to families of the NY Firefighters who perished in the Trade Towers and have brought comfort to families who lost ones in the tragedy.

To schedule an interview with Susan Gilbert,
please contact her publicist,
Penny Sansevieri at (858) 560-0121

19

Postcards

*O*ne of the most important tools in my marketing package is a simple but stunning postcard. The front of the postcard is a copy of my book cover and the back can say whatever you want. The initial batch was printed with an announcement on the back heralding the arrival of *Get Published Today!* Then, once that initial push was over, I had another batch printed with blank backs to use as thank you notes or whatever my little marketing heart desired. I would use these postcards for everything; I'd even have some special ones printed for book signings. The key here is consistency. You'll begin to develop a color scheme for your media package. I try to stay away from the formal and depressing black. Also, I would stick a copy of the postcard to the front of the folder and suddenly I had what looked like a very well thought-out and expensive kit. It was fun, colorful and informative. Something I would also use the postcards for is to announce my media kit's arrival. Several days prior to the mailing, I would send out a postcard that said something like: **Be on the lookout for your media kit, arriving shortly!** Even if the post card ended up in the circular file (and I'm sure many did) they would remember the cover of the book, and when it arrived, there would be an immediate sense of recognition. Even if the individual still had no idea what the book was about or if they even wanted to review it, they would remember it. In most cases, the announcement postcard was not the only form of advertising material they would receive from me. So again, when you're designing your marketing package, don't forget the all-important postcard. It's a vital and inexpensive part of your marketing campaign.

One final marketing tidbit…

…did you know that contrary to popular belief it's the back of your postcard that gets the most attention not the front? You have exactly three seconds to impress someone with whatever slogan or pitch before they'll turn the postcard over and look at the picture on the front.

Marketing Tip:

Don't ever send one single bit of correspondence without including a piece of marketing material, a bookmark or business card. Even include a bookmark when you pay your bills. Hey, your creditors always fill their envelopes with advertising, right? So why can't you?

*

20

Let's Review

*T*here's not enough I can say about reviews. This is a vital part of your marketing and should not be overlooked. And while there is no such thing as free advertising, this comes darned close. For the cost of an advanced review copy or a book, you can garner a review (maybe several) that will begin to open doors for you. Even bad reviews can help you. I remember when *Chicken Soup for the Soul* came out and the New York *Times* gave it a pretty bad review and look what happened. You can't walk into a bookstore without seeing stacks and stacks of some sort of "Chicken Soup" book. There are so many editions now, I've lost count. So if you get a bad review, don't despair. Cash registers still sing even if the review is negative.

Most first-time authors cannot afford to run ads in newspapers, nor should they. Buying ad space is largely ineffective and can come across as being gimmicky. An unbiased review can garner you media attention like nothing else, especially if you hit the big time with a larger publication.

There are two types of reviews. The first of which is referred to as a pre-publication review. These reviewers will expect to see galley* copies of your book. If your galley still has typos in it or doesn't have an index yet, not to worry.

Reviewers know they are advanced copies and expect that. There are several ways to produce galleys. My two favorite are either to print them myself and take them to a copy center for binding, or, contact Crane at (508) 760-1601. Crane specializes in galley printing and can do as few as ten or as many as several thousand copies. Call them for a quote, though last time I checked, they were about $10 per copy. Although the cover on your review copy does not have to be the actual cover of your book, I recommend that you include a sample copy of what the cover will look like. On the inside of the actual galley cover, though, you're going to want to include the following: title, author, publisher, publisher's phone, publisher's URL, publication date, ISBN number (get that from your publisher) and the price of the book.

Now that your galley is ready, you're going to need to send it out to many, many reviewers.

Marketing Tip

If you're sending review copies, I'd advise you *not* to mail these between the days of November 15th through December 27th as they might instead wind up as holiday gifts and never get reviewed.

❧

Timing Is Everything

Believe it or not, the day your book arrives on the reviewers desk can actually make a difference and even increase (or decrease) your chances for review. According to Jim Cox of *Midwest Book Review* (www.midwestbookreview.com),"Mondays are consistently the heaviest intake day for review copies. This is because

---

*a printed copy of your book, neatly bound

UPS does not deliver on Saturday, and neither the UPS or the Post Office deliver on Sundays. So the books that are in the UPS and Post Office pipelines over the weekend all show up added to the normal Monday intake. As the week progresses, the flow of books tends to die down a little, with Saturday (and only the Post Office delivering) tending to be the least numbers of books arriving. But countering that low Saturday figure is that while the book bags will be opened, it's fairly frequent that the books themselves will simply be stacked and added to the Monday piles before starting through the process of examination to determine their status with respect to the review selection routine."

That said, the two best days for your book to arrive on a reviewer's desk are Thursday or Friday. The competition of your books arriving decreases as the week progresses. There's really no way to ensure that the Post Office will deliver when you hope unless you get three day, or overnight delivery. If you're not sure about the time frame for delivery these days, have a the tracking feature added to a few of your packages to see when they arrive.

Now as far as months go, generally January and February tend to be the best months for review submission. According to Jim Cox, the months to avoid are October & November with people gearing up for the holiday season when bookstores make up to half or more of their entire annual sales figures. The second worst months are April & May. This is because they are the "hump months" for the Spring Season releases for the big guys who have distinct Spring & Fall Seasons to their marketing. Besides January and February, the best months or, "slump months" as most reviewers refer them to, are March, June, July & August.

Your advanced copies are going to go to the following reviewers:

Prepublication Reviewers:

Publishers Weekly

Forecasts
245 W. 17th Street
New York, NY 10011
www.publishersweekly.com
selfpub@cahners.com
(212) 463-6758 Phone
(212) 463-6631 Fax

According to a recent E-mail I received from them, *Publishers Weekly* is accepting submissions of author-subsidized works for possible review. They define author-subsidized works as those on which authors incur a fee for publication. Such titles may be print-on-demand or traditional subsidized titles. When submitting materials to them, it is essential that you follow these guidelines:

Only titles written for adults will be considered at this time.

These guidelines do not apply to children's titles.

Never send them a complete book unless you have been specifically asked to do so. Please note that a request to see a full manuscript in no way guarantees that they will run a review of that title.

You may send them a brief description/summary of the work pasted into the main body of an E-mail along with the equivalent of a cover letter.

Authors should list previous published works, if any.

Be sure to include the work's category designation (fiction, mystery, science fiction/fantasy/horror, nonfiction, lifestyles).

They would also like to see the first few (1-3) pages as a writing sample. Please either attach this as a Word rich text format file, provide a link to a web site on which they can read the sample or include it in the body of the message.

If PW is interested in considering your book for possible review, they will contact you directly and request further information.

All correspondence should be addressed to selfpub@ cahners.com, including any correspondence with individual Forecasts editors, who may write to you from other addresses.

ForeWord Magazine
Book Review Editor
Alex Moore
129 1/2 East Front Street
Traverse City, MI 49684
www.forewordmagazine.com
Reviews@foreword.com E-mail
(231) 933-3699

ForeWord Magazine is a monthly trade review journal covering independent and university presses which provides a news and review vehicle for booksellers, librarians and publishing professionals. Among the 500+ books the magazine receives each month, the editors select 40–60 for review. Books chosen for pre-publication review by Review Editor Alex Moore, represent the season's most worthy materials. The choices range from original paperbacks, hardcover, audio and electronic books. The books represent the output of independent and university press publishers, large and small. Books are selected for their potential interest to a trade buying audience. About 40% of *ForeWord* subscribers are acquisition directors at libraries; about 40% of readers are trade booksellers, encompassing chain and independent retail outlets; and another 20% are in the industry, including publishers, agents, and association professionals. *ForeWord* reviews are used by booksellers and librarians to make purchasing decisions from the universe of independently published materials flooding the marketplace. *ForeWord* does not review textbooks, technical or specialized works (particularly those directed at a professional audience), or books in languages other than English. They do consider bilingual editions and books previously published abroad if they are being released here for the first time and have a U.S. distributor. Materials must be sent three to four months in advance of publication date to be considered for review or mention. Galleys are suitable materials to send. *ForeWord* generally avoids reviewing books later than date of publication, though they do make exceptions for children's and audio books. Authors who want to know if their submissions have been received should E-mail reviews@forewordmagazine.com a few days after their estimated day of arrival. To find out if a book is going to be reviewed, E-mail reviews@forewordmagazine.com, 45 days after the submission's arrival.

Library Journal
Book Review Editor
245 W. 17th Street
New York, NY 10011-5300
http://libraryjournal.reviewsnews.com/
(212) 463-6818 Phone
(212) 463-6734 Fax

The *Library Journal* is a magazine geared to public libraries. Of the 30,000 books they receive, they will usually review 4,500 each year. A good review by The LJ might move between 1,000 to 5,000 copies of your book. Books are selected for their potential interest to a broad spectrum of libraries. About 50% of LJ's readers are in public libraries; another 21% are in academic libraries; about 13% are in special libraries; and about 6% are in school libraries. Their reviews are used primarily by librarians to make their purchasing decisions.

Only a few areas of publishing fall outside LJ's scope: textbooks, children's books, very technical or specialized works (particularly those directed at a professional audience), and books in languages other than English. They will consider bilingual editions, and have a quarterly review of Spanish-language books.

Books previously published abroad are eligible if they are being released here for the first time and have a U.S. distributor.

Recently, The *Library Journal* has begun accepting print-on-demand books. This came directly from their web site:

We do consider print-on-demand and on-line materials, but we would like to see these materials as much in advance of the launch date as possible. For print-on-demand books, please send us proofs as soon as they are available and specify estimated launch date as well as ISBN, price, and other relevant material, as with any traditional book. Include the following information: Author, title; name, address, and telephone number of publisher; date of publication; price; number of pages; and ISBN and LC numbers if available. Please indicate whether any illustrations, an index, or bibliography will be included; also include a brief description of the book, its intended audience, and information on the author's background.

Book Magazine
Reviews Editor
252 West 37th Street, 5th Floor
New York, NY 10018
www.bookmagazine.com/

Send galleys two to three months prior to your pub date.

New York Times Book Reviews
Charles McGrath
229 W. 43rd Street
New York, NY 10036
www.nytimes.com/books
(212) 556-1234 Phone
(212) 556-7088 Fax

Send galleys two to three months prior to your pub date. Send a finished copy of the book once it's available.

Independent Publisher On-line
New Title Listings
400 W. Front St. 4A
Traverse City, MI 49684
www.independentpublisher.com
(231) 933-0445
val@bookpublishing.com

Independent Publisher On-line Magazine is published monthly on the Web at www.independentpublisher.com, and reviews books produced by independent, university and small press publishers. Submitted books will go through an editorial review process. Instead of sending them to reviewers, they now prepare the listings of chosen books in-house, and post them in the IP On-line New Title Listing section for two months. Approximately 25 new titles will be chosen and added each month.

Due to the large number of buyers and rights agents that use their site to scout for prospects, New Title Listings will take a dramatic shift toward the nonfiction books these buyers are interested in. The emphasis is in the following genres:

Aging, Animals, Business, Children's, Computer/Internet, Cooking, Education, Family, Finance, Gift, Health, Home & Garden, How-To, Humor, Motivation, Nutrition, Parenting, Personal Development, Publishing, Relationships, Self Help, Reference, Writing. The genres of fiction, poetry, biography, and history are unlikely to be listed by IP On-line in the foreseeable future.

About *Independent Publisher On-line*:

This magazine is published monthly on the Web at www.independentpublisher.com, and posts new title listings of books produced by independent and university presses and self-publishers.

IP On-line lists books that they feel have viable sales potential to the agents and buyers who use our site to scout for fresh titles from independent presses. They will use the material and cover images from your own website to synopsize listed books. If you do not have title info available on the Web, please be prepared to e-mail them a synopsis and cover scan.

Independent Publisher magazine requirements:

Submit one copy of a bound galley, finished book, e-book, or book on tape. (Only first editions published in the current calendar year will be considered. The key is when the book is published, not necessarily the copyright date.)

Submitted books must include:

Title; Authors; Publisher; Address; Phone; website; Price; Cover Style; Page Count; ISBN #; Publication Month and Year.

Independent Publisher On-line does not accept unbound galleys, periodicals, or videotapes.

IP On-line accepts no responsibility for lost or stolen submissions, and does not notify publishers of books not selected for listing. If a self-addressed stamped postcard is included, every effort will be made to complete and return it.

All books become the property of *Independent Publisher On-line* and are eventually donated to non-profit organizations.

Questions? Contact Jim Barnes at jimb@bookpublishing.com

The Village Voice
Lenora Todaro
36 Cooper Square
New York, NY 10003

The *Village Voice* considers reviews for literary fiction and literary, illustrated, political, and topical nonfiction. They rarely but occasionally review genre fiction and children's literature; they almost never review self-help or business books. Take a look at recent issues (you can read them on-line at www.villagevoice.com) and determine whether your book seems appropriate for their section.

They prefer to receive galleys at least two months before the publication date. If that isn't possible, or if galleys aren't available, send them the finished book, along with a press release containing any pertinent information. They also say that fancy press kits and author photos aren't necessary and won't impact their decision-making process.

If you have a New York reading in the near future, send a press release at least two weeks beforehand to:

Grace Bastidas
Listings Department
Village Voice
36 Cooper Square
New York, NY 10003

You can also fax press releases on readings to Bastidas at 212-475-5807.

As with most reviewers, don't call the *Voice* repeatedly and ask whether they received your book or press release, and whether they know yet what issue you'll be reviewed in. If you sent it, the odds are pretty good they received it. The odds are also good that, since they get about 200 books every week, they haven't read it yet. But they do promise to make their effort to look at every book and press release they receive.

If they review your book in the book section or the literary supplement, they will send you a copy of the review once it appears. If you want to double check if your book has been reviewed, you can also go to www.villagevoice.com, and type your name into the search engine. Maybe you'll be surprised.

Chicago Tribune Books
Elizabeth Taylor (etaylor@tribune.com)

435 N. Michigan Avenue
Chicago, IL 60611
http://chicagotribune.com/features/books/
(312) 222-3232 Phone

They review galleys two to three months prior to the publication date, then send them a finished copy of your book. Elizabeth is very busy; only E-mail her to check receipt of the book or for some other important issue.

The American Book Review

Rebecca Kaiser, Managing Editor
Illinois State University
Campus Box 4241
Normal, IL 61790-4241
(309) 438-3026
rakaise@ilstu.edu

The American Book Review is an internationally circulated bi-monthly print journal that specializes in reviews of frequently neglected published works of fiction, poetry, and literary criticism from small, regional, university, ethnic, avant-garde, and women's presses. ABR as a literary journal aims to project the sense of engagement that writers themselves feel about what is being published.

They do not review non-literary works, which concerns such subjects as self-help, health, or how-to. You may send all review copies (galleys are fine). They will consider books within six months of their publication dates. Follow-up inquiries can be made to the e-mail address listed above.

Ruminator Review

Margaret Todd Maitland, Editor
1648 Grand Avenue

St. Paul, MN 55105
http://ruminator.com/hmr/
(651) 699-2610 Phone
(651) 699-0970 Fax
review@hungrymind.com

They review both galleys three to four months prior to the pub date. Their magazine (*The Ruminator Review*) is releases quarterly to 30,000 subscribers and sold in 350 books stores.

Romantic Times Magazine
Small Press Reviewer
55 Bergen Street
Brooklyn, NY 11201
www.romantictimes.com
(718) 237-1097 Phone
rtinfo@romantictimes.com

They will only review galleys. Besides romance they also review mystery and science fiction novels. Also, it's worth noting, they give review consideration first to those authors who have placed ads with the magazine.

Post-Publication Reviewers

Once your book has rolled off of the presses, it's time to send out more review copies. I recommend sending a copy of the book along with a media kit.

Midwest Book Review
James A. Cox
278 Orchard Drive
Oregon, WI 53575
www.midwestbookreviews.com

(608) 835-7937 Phone

They review about 450 books each month out of the 1,500 they receive. James Cox says they will consider any book as long as it's in finished form. Send a copy of your book and press release. He says he prefers not getting an entire media kit.

Amazon Book Reviews
Editorial Department
Post Office Box 81226
Seattle, WA 98108-1226
www.amazon.com

They prefer finished copies, but I'd call and check with them to find out specific departments to address this to, based on your genre. They are revising this process as of this writing, so it's best to check with them to get the most current information. You can reach them at (206) 266-2952.

Rowse Reviews
John Culleton, Editor
2401 Haight Avenue
Eldersburg, MD 21784
www.wexfordpress.com/
rowse@wexfordpress.com

Rowse Reviews says they encourage self-published works and small presses. I've taken the following from their web site and I believe this describes best what they do: "*Rowse Reviews* is a monthly review covering most genres. A major goal is to create legitimate review copy for authors that need such. Self-published and small-press offerings are especially welcome." Clearly, they aim to be author-friendly as well as reader-friendly. Their circulation at this point is limited to library systems in Maryland. They don't review religious/inspirational tracts, new age, pornography, poetry, family memoirs or cookbooks. They won't deal with electronic text submitted in word processor format. They review finished works, not manuscripts. Galley proofs are okay. Not every work merits a review, and not every review will be favorable.

USA Today
Carol Memmott, Book Editor
7950 Jones Branch Drive
McLean, VA 22107
www.usatoday.com
(703) 276-3400

A finished book should be sent to them one month before the pub date.

LA Times Book Magazine
Attn: Steve Wasserman
Times Mirror Square
Los Angeles, CA 90053
www.latimes.com
(213) 237-2547

Send finished books no further out than three months past the pub date.

New York Review of Books
Robert Silvers
1755 Broadway, Floor 5
New York, NY 10019
www.nybooks.com
(212) 757-8070 Phone
(212) 333-5374 Fax

They review finished books only. Not too far from the pub date is always preferred. This is a biweekly magazine that publishes reviews, excerpts, and will also buy serial rights. Their circulation is 130,000 and they review 400 books each year.

On-Line Review Sites

- Bookreporter.com—Aside from their review staff, members of their site are also welcome to post reviews of the books they are currently reading.
- Salon.com—Offers review sites, you can try to sell your freelance work here.
- BookZone.com has a myriad of review sites for you to choose from. Just plug in your category and out will come a list of book reviewers for your genre.

Final reminder!

When submitting materials for review, don't forget to include the following information: Author, title; name, address, and telephone number of publisher; date of publication; price; number of pages; and ISBN number. Please indicate whether any illustrations, an index, or bibliography will be included; also include a brief description of the book, its intended audience, and information on the author's background.

21

Niche reviews

$\mathcal{B}$esides the standard review markets, you might want to consider garnering more niche reviews. Once you've figured out who your specific audience is, you can target your book for niche reviews. For example, is your book on European travel? Check the travel section of your local paper and see if there's a spot for your book. In our Sunday paper there is a whole travel section complete with travel advice and articles (hint, hint). There are hundreds of syndicated columnists, reporters and editors that have newspaper space to fill. Last year, I was working on getting reviews for *A Dance in the Desert*, a book about one man's struggle with epilepsy. Given the subject of the book, I went to nationwide Epilepsy foundations and asked if they would review the book for their newsletters and magazines. In so doing, we captured an audience either directly or indirectly affected by this disease who were interested in her book. Find out who your audience is, then study the various publications and target them for a copy of your book. If you're looking for a list of syndicated columnists nationwide, try *Editor & Publisher*. They do an issue in August that classifies columnists by subject matter. The cost for this is $8.50 and can be obtained by checking out their web site at www.

editorandpublisher.com, or by calling (212) 675-4380. Now, what about the magazine market? When I began to research this market I was astounded to find out how many different magazines there were that I had never even heard of. Did you write something on the mining industry? How about contacting someone at *Coal Age* to see if they're interested in looking at your book. Is your book animal related? How about *Reptile Fancy* or *Ferret Fancy* (by the same company that does *Cat Fancy*). See what I mean? Get on your browser and type in "magazine" you'll be amazed at what comes up.

More Directories and Alternative Review Sources:

- **Senior Media Directory** (702) 786-7419—they list magazines, newsletters and newspapers geared to the senior market.
- **QBR: The Black Book Review**, Max Rodriguez, Publisher, 9 West 126th Street, 2nd Floor, New York, NY 10027; 212-348-1681; Fax: 212-427-9901. Web: http://www.qbr. com. A review of African American books is published six times per year.
- **Books & Culture: A Christian Book Review**, John Wilson, Editor, 465 Gundersen Drive, Carol Stream IL 60188; 630-260-6200; Fax: 630-260-0114. This bimonthly magazine reviews books on science, politics, culture, fiction, etc. from a Christian perspective. Circulation: 16,000.
- **New Age Retailer**, Continuity Publishing, 1300 N. State Street #105, Bellingham, WA 98225; 360-676-0789; 800-463-9243; Fax: 360-676-0932. E-mail: mail@ newageretailer.com. Web: http://www.newageretailer. com. Ray Hemachandra, Book Review Editor; ext. 3013; E-mail: ray@newageretailer.com.

- **Travel Books Worldwide**, Peter Manston, Editor, 2510 S Street, P.O. Box 162266, Sacramento, CA 95816; 916-452-5200.
- **NAPRA ReVIEW**, 109 North Beach Road, P.O. Box 9, Eastsound, WA 98245; 360-376-2702; 800-367-1907; Fax: 360-376-2704. E-mail: napra@napra.com. Web: http://www.napra.com. Michael Weaver, Book Review Editor; Antoinette Botsford, Children's Book Editor.
- **Black Issues Book Review**, Empire State Building #7720, 350 Fifth Avenue, New York, NY 10018; 212-947-8794; Fax: 212-947-5674. E-mail: bibookreview@cmbiccw.com. Web: http://www. bibookreview.com. Samiya Bashir, Reviews Editor. Publication office: 10520 Warwick Avenue #B-8, Fairfax VA 22030; 703-385-2981; Fax: 703-385-1839.
- **Feminist Bookstore News**, P.O. Box 882554, San Francisco, CA 94188; 415-642-9993; Fax: 415-642-9995. E-mail: fbn@fembknews.com. Carol Seajay, Editor.
- **Science Fiction Chronicle**, Andrew Porter, Editor, P.O. Box 022730, Brooklyn, NY 11202-0056; 718-643-9011; Fax: 718-522-3308. E-mail: sf_chronicle@compuserve.com.
- **Sci/Tech Book News**, Jane Erskine, Managing Editor, 5739 N.E. Sumner Street, Portland, OR 97218; 503-281-9230; Fax: 503-287-4485. E-mail: booknews@booknews.com.
- **Association of Alternative News Weeklies**, 1000 Connecticut Avenue N.W. #822, Washington DC 20036; 202-822-1955; Fax: 202-822-0929.
- **Parenting Publications of America**, 1846 Lockhill-Selma Road #102, San Antonio, TX 78213; 210-348-8396; Fax: 210-348-8397. E-mail: parpubs@family.com. "Our list of members is available for a one time fee of $200 which includes unlimited updated lists. We have 151 member

publications, all regional parenting publications, with a combined circulation of 6.7 million."

These sites are courtesy of John Kremer. Need more review sites? Take a look at John Kremer's web site at www. bookmarket.com and click on Major Newspaper book reviewers.

Mock Reviews

I've said it before, and I'll say it again: Make the life of your media contact or your book review contact as easy as possible. This includes slipping a mock review into your media kit. Put together a flattering blurb about your book and include it in your package. More often than not, the reviewer will end up using the review you've already written.

Following Up

After ten days to two weeks, follow up with the reviewer to see if your book has been selected for review. Keep this conversation brief and know that you might be making the same call ten times until you get an answer. First, you want to introduce yourself and let them know you are calling to confirm that they received your book (mention the title). If they say they haven't received it, offer to call back in a week. Reviewers often get five crates of books to review each day. As you can imagine, this takes a while to sift through. If the reviewer has received your book, ask him or her what the status is with regard to the review process. If they tell you that it has been selected for review, inquire as to when a review could be expected, and check to see if there is anything else they require from you. Thank them before hanging up. If it has not yet been scheduled for review, ask them if there is anything else they need to make their decision. Suggest calling them back in a week or two (get the best day and time to call), thank them and hang up. Don't keep them on the phone with pressing questions about their time frame. Do take copious notes and keep a log handy of when you called and what transpired during the contact. Each time you phone a reviewer you need to sound fresh, happy and accommodating to their needs. If the book isn't right for them or they won't review it for whatever reason, thank them politely and move on to your next reviewer.

A Final Word on Reviews

Encourage anyone and everyone who has access to a computer to review you on Amazon and Barnes & Noble. Offer them a second book discounted (or free) for them to give away. Then get the name of the person they gave that book to, and follow up with them. Get them to review it, as well. Have you ever been perusing a book on Amazon with no reviews? How motivated were you to buy it? Unless you already knew you wanted it, most people require a bit more convincing than that.

If you do a lot of shopping on Amazon, consider reviewing books in your category or genre (you are reading the competition, aren't you?). If you notice on Amazon you can review, and, if you're registered, it will produce a link to your book. So help out the competition by submitting a review and spread the word about your book in the process.

Tip!

Looking for more reviewers? Then head on over to BookZonePro where you'll find a free searchable database of reviewers: www.bookzonepro.com.

22

Thinking Outside Of The Bookstore Box!

I don't know about you, but when I first got published, one of my all-time aspirations was to see my book in a bookstore window. When I found out that most bookstores can't or won't carry your print-on-demand publication, I was devastated. But after speaking with many small publishers, I realized I wasn't alone. The fact of the matter is, large publishing houses will actually purchase space on bookstore shelves thereby virtually guaranteeing you a spot. Next time you walk through a bookstore, take a look at the placement of books. Have you ever wondered by some books end up on the promotions table right as you're walking through the door? Or why some get front row exposure on end-caps? It's not because some nice salesperson put them there. It's because a publisher bought space in those areas. This doesn't mean that you won't ever get your book into stores; you will probably succeed in placing them locally. As far as nationwide exposure goes though, that probably won't come until you've built some momentum for your book.

If statistics are any guide though, it's fair to say that bookstores aren't the only ticket in town. In fact, according to the Book Industry Study Group (BISG), bookstores accounted for 35% of retail sales in the United States in 1998; the remaining 65% of the retail market is now divided among mass-market retailers, mail-order, book clubs, specialty stores, and on-line booksellers. This means that even though bookstores seem like the logical place to carry your book, most people who have reached success have done so by thinking outside the bookstore box. Since you aren't publishing traditionally, you shouldn't consider marketing traditionally either. Pam Hansell, of Inkspot, suggests the following: "Think small. Odd advice, but effective. When I marketed academic books, many of the most successful titles never appeared in splashy *New York Times Book Review* ads or made it to a bookstore shelf. Instead we isolated the target market and promoted the book to that very specific audience. Self-published authors don't have the advantage of a large marketing budget so they must make certain each promotional effort is targeted. Being creative is also an important thing self-published authors can do. Before he became a best-selling author, E. Lynn Harris left copies of his self-published books in beauty salons. Why beauty salons? Because at the salon people have a lot of time to read. He had a built-in audience and was able to cultivate a loyal following. That's creative (and smart) marketing." Jim Donovan, author of *Handbook to a Happier Life*, struggled with the same challenge when he was marketing his book. "I decided to approach a pet store that I frequented to see if they would carry the book." Donovan said. Since his book was not animal related, I asked him why a pet store? His answer was simple: "I have no competition." The book is displayed at the register, and does very well. "Don't get caught

Did you know?

The five reasons people buy in bookstores:

- *Reviews, publicity*
- *Recommendations*
- *Browsing*
- *Window displays, end caps or face-out books*
- *Staff recommendations*

§

up in bookstore sales," says Donovan, "thirty-five percent of the American population has never even been in a bookstore." Give some thought for a moment as to where else you might see books. How about a museum, or an amusement park or even a national park. What about office supply stores, gas stations, travel stores, empowerment stores (Successories), record stores, wineries, children's stores, home stores, day spas or beauty salons, novelty shops, kitchen and cooking stores (Williams-Sonoma). Get the picture? There are hundreds upon hundreds of alternative spots to carry your book. These are only just a few. I'm certain you can think of many more.

Now, this doesn't mean you should ignore the bookstore idea altogether. As a matter of fact, when you're out and about you should always make it a point to drop into any bookstore you run across. Introduce yourself to the store manager or community relations manager and hand them a copy of your book. It's even more impressive if you have a press kit already made up, too. Even if you don't have a copy of your book with you (shame on you) make sure to carry some business cards, book marks or postcards. Don't even think of going in there without leaving something behind! You should get to know your area bookstores and offer to come in there and sign books, do a reading or host a seminar. Give them something to give their customers. Even if they can't stock your book in their store, they might consider hosting a signing anyway, just to support a local writer. Most bookstores are very good about supporting their community. And if they're not interested right away (their event calendars fill up very quickly) they might be interested later on down the road, so make sure to keep in touch with them.

23

Book Clubs

Getting into a book club means the kind of exposure you can't get anywhere else. If you've ever belonged to a book club, you know that they send you a catalog each month and you have to send back their form if you don't want the selection of the month. Otherwise, it's automatically sent to you. Whoever came up with that was brilliant!

In days-gone-by book clubs were the ideal way to reach people in remote areas or avid readers too busy to spend an afternoon in a bookstore. Book clubs were made attractive with deals, bonus points and free books just for signing up. But with the advent of the Internet, all of that is beginning to change. First of all, on-line bookstores like Barnes & Noble and Amazon are the solution to those unable to get to the bookstore; they can shop in their bunny slippers. The Internet has also, in a sense, raised the bar on offers, pricing and service. Book clubs are going on-line now so members don't have to hassle with envelopes and postage. And if you've ever been a member of a book club you know that customer service was probably the last thing on their list. Well, not anymore. The Net has forced them to be more responsive, and in a sense, breathed new life into these American institutions.

In March of 2000, the nations two oldest book clubs joined forces. Book of the Month Club and The Literary Guild once arch rivals competing over deals, authors and books were now on the same team and Bookspan was born. According to some recent statistics, this partnership encompasses more than forty clubs with access to ten million active members. President and CEO, Markus Wilhelm, believes that in the next couple of years they could be looking at over one hundred clubs total.

Given this history, you can imagine that going forward, the doors will open for a variety of new clubs and catalogs. Imagine what this could mean for book sales.

Guidelines for clubs are simple. Send a finished copy of your book. They don't want manuscripts, they want published books. According to some updated information I've received, they buy from both traditional houses and small presses. In fact, they encourage small press submissions and love discovering exciting new authors. Submit your sample to them along with a cover letter indicating the estimated pub date (if you haven't passed it yet), book price, page count, a brief description of the book, summary of its content and the number and type of illustrations. It's also helpful to send photocopies of sample illustrations and an author bio (noting any previous books). Package all of this up and send it to the book club that you feel best fits your audience.

BookSpan
1271 Avenue of the Americas
3rd Floor
New York, NY 10020-9991

The following clubs are all part of the BookSpan group and have the same mailing address. Send it to the attention of the Editor at the specific club you're targeting:

- Book of the Month Club—Arthur Goldwag
- Quality Paperback Book Club—David Roth-Ey
- Children's Book of the Month Club—Kate Winchester
- History Book Club—John Major
- Jewish Book Club—Arthur Goldwag
- One Spirit Book Club—Jane Perkins
- Crafter's Choice—BJ Berti, Editorial Director
- Country Homes and Gardens—Denise McGann, Editorial Director
- DoubleDay Book Club—Nancy Whilin
- Rhapsody Book Club—Nancy Whilin
- Venus Book Club—Nancy Whilin
- The Literary Guild—Nancy Whilin
- Science Fiction—Nancy Whilin
- Mystery Book Club—Nancy Whilin

The phone number to reach them for any questions related to the submission process can be directed to: (212) 522-4200. Their web site address is: www.booksonline.com. You won't find any information here for submitting your book for consideration, but you can get a good idea of the books they already offer in their various clubs.

Got Books?

Last year, I got 100 copies of my book, *The Cliffhanger*, with misprinted covers. I couldn't resell them, so they sat boxed up in my office. I tried organizing a book signing for charity but the idea never got off the ground. I was finally referred to The Friends of the Library. They take used books and resell them, the proceeds benefit your local library. Some are even given to the homeless. What a great cause! If you have some books you need to get rid of, don't hang onto them the way I did—get in touch with your local branch of Friends of the Library and donate them. And, if you're interested in finding a great sale on used books, head on over to www.booksalefinder.com. This site lists all library-related sale events in your area.

❧

24

Catalog Sales

$\mathcal{E}$very year, each of us receives on average 78 catalogs and ninety three percent of us end up ordering from them (I know I do). Each year, over $93 billion in merchandise is sold through the catalog industry. If you have a book that would sell well in a specific catalog, you might want to think seriously about approaching this market. You may have to give them a fairly deep discount, but think of it this way. If you're picked up by a catalog it could mean moving 1,000 to 40,000 books annually. Sound appealing? Then read on.

It's advisable that you approach them as early as possible. Most companies will begin filling a catalog six months prior to mailing. Some companies begin filling them sooner than that. You'll want to contact the individual companies to get their submission forms and find out what their policy is as it relates to POD. Most catalog companies buy non-returnable which is perfect for you, but since there are so many different catalogs out there, you'll want to check this first.

Figure out which catalogs would work best with your product then submit to them all at once. With your submission package you should include a well-crafted sales letter along with a handy sales blurb for their catalog. Again, the more work you do for them, the easier you will make their job.

You should plan to follow up on your submission about two weeks after you mailed it. Do not inquire whether or not they will carry it, just ask them if they got it. It will take about six weeks for them to respond back to you as to whether they will carry it or not. Sometimes they will try your book on a test run (500 to 1000 copies) which is fine. If they do contact you, stay in touch with your publisher and let them know what's going on. If you do get an initial order you'll want to make sure to turn it around as quickly as possible. You're going to want to discuss (and possibly negotiate) who gets to pay for shipping. Most of the time the catalog company will pay your shipping costs, but if they don't, you'll want to figure this out before striking a deal. If you get a large order, you may even be able to talk your publisher into footing the bill for shipping. You might also want to discuss this with your publisher prior to submitting your book for consideration. If they are not open to the idea of your book selling through a catalog (hard to believe, I know, but it could happen), then you want to know this in advance. This way you can either switch to a publisher who would consider it, or forget about the catalog market altogether.

Depending on the catalog(s) you are targeting, your window of opportunity will vary. Generally, catalog companies will buy during two seasons. For a September catalog the negotiations need to be completed by the end of July. For a Spring catalog, negotiations will need to be completed by December 1. Not all companies adhere to this purchasing window and some even buy their product up to eight times a year.

Catalog Directories

There are over 7,000 catalogs published in the United States alone. To get an idea of the types of catalogs out there, take a moment to peruse the sites listed below. If cataloging is going to be your primary focus, you might want to think about investing in a directory of catalogs. Before you do though, check to see if your local library carries these (most of them do). For the cost of an afternoon and a couple of rolls of coins (for copies) you could get all the information you need without footing a big bill. Otherwise, you can go on-line and order free catalogs from some of the places listed below.

The Directory of Mail Order Catalogs
(800) 562-2139
www.greyhouse.com

Their directories used to be available in book form, but after perusing their web site, I think they only deal with on-line information. Their on-line subscription, while very thorough, is kind of pricey.

Catalog Handbook
(414) 272-9977

You can get this magazine at Borders, Barnes & Noble, Crown Books and Waldens Books. At $5.99 it's a pretty good deal.

The following is a list of on-line resources for finding and ordering copies of catalogs you want to consider for your book.

Shop at Home Catalogs
www.shopathome.com
Check out their web site and order some of their catalogs on-line. Some of them have a minimal charge, but most are free.

The Catalog Shop
www.thecatalogshop.com

Another great place to order catalogs. Most of these are free.

The Mall of Catalogs
www.mallofcatalogs.com

They have a very diverse selection of catalogs to chose from. Again, these are either free or at a minimal cost to you.

Buyer's Index
www.buyersindex.com

This site will lead you to the individual catalog companies. A bit tricky to navigate though.

Catalog City
www.catalogcity.com

You can peruse each catalog on-line to get an idea of the merchandise they carry.

Catalog Link
www.cataloglink.com

Here you can order a catalog or get redirected to the catalog web site. A great resource.

Major Catalog Companies

Lillian Vernon
Winnie Lee, Buyer
One Theall
Rye, NY 10580
(914) 925-1200
www.lillianvernon.com

According to Winnie, they don't carry too many books but are open to looking at yours if it fits with their catalog. She indicated that they don't have specific buying times and are constantly updating their catalogs. Send them a price sheet, a sample of your book, and all other pertinent information we discussed earlier.

Miles Kimball
Christine Peterson
41 West 8th Avenue
Oshkosh, WI 54901
(920) 231-3800
www.mileskimball.com

Christine is the book buyer for Miles Kimball and she said that they do not discriminate against self-published authors. As a matter of fact, as long as the book meets the needs of their customers, she's very excited to discover new talent. Submit your book information sheet, the wholesale pricing, a brief book synopsis (if warranted) and an author bio.

Target Direct
1000 Westgate Drive
St. Paul, MN 55114
(651) 659-3700
(651) 637-4701 Merchandising Department
www.signals.com
www.seasonsshop.com
www.wirelesstoo.com

Target Direct now owns all three catalog companies and does their merchandising from one central location. Their recorded message says not to send samples unless requested, and list the category (Books) clearly on the outside of the package. They like the new and unique and are open to self-published authors as well as those published traditionally. Please include the price for your book, any cover samples or photographs and the publication date. They take about three months to process your package and will get back to you only if they're interested in listing your product.

25

Celebrity Endorsements

It's a known fact that one complimentary nod from a famous face can launch even the most obscure product. Most advertising agencies pay a high price to have a celebrity take a swig of their soft drink or wear a pair of their running shoes. The good news is, if you can get an endorsement for your book it probably won't cost you a thing, except maybe time, patience, persistence and oh, did I mention patience? It's a long road to get an endorsement, but once traveled can prove very profitable to the sale of your book. The first thing you have to remember is that when you're trying to get a celebrity to endorse your book, they're doing you a huge favor. Contact them in the way they wish to be contacted (mail, e-mail or fax) follow their guidelines (or more than likely the guidelines their agency dictates) to the letter. Now, your celebrity endorsement might not be from the hottest celebrity. It might a radio personality, a local celebrity, or an author. Who your chosen celebrities are will likely depend on your book. First of all, you're going to want to contact those celebs who have a vested interest in your topic—that will help to greatly increase your chances of getting a response.

When you're putting together your list of desired endorsements, start with a long list of people—say twenty or so. One by one, some of these celebs might fall off "No interest" or "On location" are the two biggest reasons I encounter.

So, let's say that the target of your endorsement is an actor, you'll want to start by contacting The Screen Actor's Guild to get their current agent/publicist information. You can do this by calling: (323) 549-6737 if the celeb you're looking for is LA based. If not, head on over to www.sag.org for the current contact information for their New York office. If you're trying to reach an author, your best bet will be to head on over to their web site, determine who their publisher is and call them. Sometimes the publisher will filter these requests, sometimes the author has a separate agent who will handle this. Sometimes author information can be tough to come by. If you're pursuing someone with obscure contact information, try sending your request to The Author's Guild, if they're a member The Guild will have their current contact information. You can send an e-mail to staff@authorsregistry.org with you list of names.

Once you've gotten contact information for all of your endorsement hopefuls, you'll want to get your package ready to send to them. Some people will want to see a synopsis, outline or press release. Whatever they ask for, make sure it's ready to send off to them right away. The last thing you need is a delay in getting information out to them. You will be requested to mail, e-mail or fax a synopsis and be asked to check back. You'll want to wait a few days to confirm their receipt of this information. At that time, you might get a response "We'll forward this on" or "Sorry, Mr. Such and Such doesn't endorse this type of material." At that point (or later if you're asked to call back), you'll be asked to send your packet. An endorsement package should include nearly the same information as your review kit: press release, book information, synopsis, book. With this, you'll also want to include a list of "sample endorsements" much like the mock reviews we discussed earlier in this book. You'll want to have something they can circle and fax or mail back to you (don't forget your FedEx envelope or SASE). Your cover letter should be professional and appreciative. Remember, they don't have to do this. It should also indicate that you will forward a copy of the final product once your book is printed and rolling off the presses. Once that package is sent, then it's time to wait and wait and wait and sometimes re-send them a package if they can't seem to locate it. All the while remember that while this process is long and arduous at times, it's worth every letter, every call and every book mailed out.

The truth of the matter is that this is sometimes the least considered marketing aspect of an author's campaign. In fact, most authors I work with never give any thought to celebrity endorsements. Even those who have spent years in the business. A good example of this is an author I have recently had the pleasure of working with. His book, *What I Learned on the Way Down*, was all about his life as an Emmy award winning writer, sky diver and personal assistant to Jerry Lewis. The last part stopped me in my tracks. When I asked my client about getting an endorsement from Mr. Lewis he looked at me as though I were speaking Greek. The thought had never occurred to him. In this case, he'd spent so much time with Mr. Lewis he simply never gave it a second thought. So, when you're figuring out ways to market your book, give some consideration to celebrity endorsements. You might even know someone who knows someone who knows someone, narrowing that six degrees of separation. If you don't, then you'll have to go about it the old fashioned way. In either case, getting even one famous face to acknowledge your work is often enough to get even the most apprehensive buyer to give your book a second look and in the end, isn't that what it's all about?

Never judge a book by its movie.

❧ J.W. Eagan

The Media

*Consider the postage stamp. It secures success through its
ability to stick to one thing until it gets there.*

*** Josh Billings**

26

Cracking The Code

Getting into the media spotlight may seem at times like cracking
some secret code. It's not easy, I'll grant you that, and it does
require persistence the likes of which you've never seen. It takes a
passion for your work, a sunny disposition when you hear "no"
and a lion's share of courage to keep pressing on when no one
seems to care that you've written a novel destined to be a classic. I
hope the information in the next several pages helps to shed a bit
of light on the elusive and all too intriguing media frenzy. But don't
stop there. I've only scratched the surface on a national level as far
as media contacts go. There are many, many more places for you
to look. Take your focus off of the national spotlight and look
around your own back yard. You probably have a local talk show,
morning show or radio program (or two) you can try to sway with
your outstanding media kit and story idea. And that's the trick.
Come up with a be-all and end-all story idea, believe in what
you're doing and pitch until you have knocked on every door
imaginable

27

Pitching Your Story Idea

*O*kay, so you've got a great book-related story idea. Now what?

Well, now it's time to begin knocking on some doors. It's time to start pitching that idea. But where and how do you begin? First, study your intended target. Watch their show, listen to their station, read their magazine or newspaper. Knowing who you're pitching to is half your battle. When you're doing this research, ask yourself what the demographic is of the viewer, listener, or reader. This will save you the cost of sending a book to someone who might not be interested. You'll also save the person at the other end the time of having to read through your material and toss your stuff in their circular file.

There's also an art to pitching effectively. First of all, when you're pitching a television show (and sometimes radio too), pitch a segment. In other words your pitch packet (or e-mail) should be a segment suggestion as opposed to a simple pitch. When pitching a segment, you'll want to keep in mind that television is a visual medium. Now, while this may sound obvious to some, you'll be surprised at how many people still pitch a dry segment. In other words, they'll suggest a segment on themselves and their book with no footage or additional guests. Shows (especially morning shows and night time programs like Dateline) don't want talking heads, it's boring and it doesn't keep the audience. You want to catch those channel surfers and get them to stop surfing and start watching. They'll take on average a second or two to decide if they want to stick around. Keep them enthralled and you've managed to capture the toughest audience.

Also when you're pitching, don't just pitch yourself. Pitch something newsworthy or controversial. If you can, try to tie your book into a news angle or a recent headline. Pitching issues is a great way to get noticed. "The biggest mistake authors make when trying to get onto major radio and TV shows," says Joan Stewart (www.publicityhound.com), "is that they pitch themselves or their book." For example, if your book is on obsessive behavior (e.g. stalking), suggest a topic that would entice them. For example, "Obsession isn't flattery." Then suggest one or two guest speakers who might bring up a controversial side of this topic. If you can package it like this, you've just helped a producer create a show and made their job easier.

Now, you're probably thinking that might be easy for a nonfiction book but what about the fiction writers in the group? Well, did you write a murder mystery? Why not pitch a story about all the unsolved murders in the United States (you'd be amazed how many of these crimes never get solved). Did you write a historical romance novel? Why not delve into the history books and uncover a real torrid love story. Get my drift? Where there's a story, there's a way. Find out what your angle is and build from there. If that angle doesn't seem to be working then create a new one. The thing is to keep trying. Good luck! If you get on national TV, I want to know about it.

Pitching via E-mail

There's been a lot of discussion lately regarding pitching E-mail and pitching traditionally. For many of us e-mail pitching is an easy, effective, and inexpensive way for us to promote. The downside to this is that many e-mail pitches have become a form of SPAM. Many reporters get upwards of three hundred plus e-mails a day,

some even get as many as a thousand. With that many e-mails filling their mailbox, one sure way to get on a reporters nerves is to send a pitch that is too long, incomplete, and untargeted. It's a fine line between e-mail pitches and spamming. Some still prefer to receive your pitch via fax. It's a good idea to double check this. Fax machines in busy studios run all day and night filling their bin with thousands of pitches. Usually, when you e-mail a pitch you're directing it to a specific person (unless your pitch is going to editor@XYZMagazine). But there's also a dark side to the electronic pitch. Recently, an author friend of mine told me he submitted a story idea to several media outlets via E-mail. And, he pitched them all at once. This means that with one click of the mouse, you can save yourself hours of faxing time, hundreds of sheets of paper and get your message out across the country, right? Wrong. Editors, reporters and news people really don't like it when you mass E-mail them. It's inconsiderate and it's annoying and it's a surefire way to get your story ignored. If you're going to pitch by E-mail and you've confirmed it with the source that they prefer an initial contact made via E-mail, then go for it. But don't mass E-mail.

Because of the extensive e-mail pitches reporters are receiving, some have begun investing in e-mail services to help them filter out unwanted mail. To avoid getting your pitch sent to the delete bin, there are a few things you can do to help position your pitch for better consideration.

- First of all, make sure you're pitching the correct person for your story. If you're not, don't ask them to forward it on to the right person. When in doubt, check their web site or call to find out where to send your pitch.
- Always put your news hook in the subject line. A news hook should be no more than three to five words. Also, include the name of your author, company, or book title beside your news hook so a busy reporter can quickly identify your e-mail. Don't send an e-mail that has this in the subject line: "News release from XYZ" and make them search through the e-mail to find your news hook. Remember, it's an e-mail pitch not a scavenger hunt.
- Always use the "above the fold" rule. This means that you make sure your pitch appears above the fold in any e-mailed (or faxed) release. Ideally, your news hook should appear in the subject line of your e-mail and then again in the first few lines of the release. If your subject line is a "teaser" then the teaser should be explained in the first few lines of your pitch. By teaser I mean for example, a line that will help pique the reporters interest. Usually a teaser line is in the form of a question. The answer to whatever question you used should then be aptly explained in the first few lines of the pitch.
- Don't send attachments! This is probably one of the biggest pet peeves of any reporter or producer. Not just because of viruses, but because it's an additional step they have to take to open your pitch.Build a press room on your web site. More and more, the media is going electronic and so should your media kit. Put the entire contents of it (media kit) on your web site and let the media peruse your bio, press releases, and book information right there on the web. Even if you pitch them electronically you can still include a short sentence to direct them to your site. For example: "For a complete

media kit, please visit: www.yourwebsite.com." But always offer to send them one in case they don't want to view it electronically.

- Don't forget your contact information. I can't tell you how many producers I've spoken with who tell me this is the first thing people forget. Don't assume that a reporter will reply to your e-mail. They may need to pick up the phone for a more immediate response. If your number isn't included, guess what? Neither is your story.

The moral of this story? Don't just point and click your way through a campaign. Instead, pretend that on each E-mail, you will be required to affix a 37-cent stamp. This alone will prevent you from sending a press release about your book signing in Milwaukee to an editor in San Diego.

Marketing Tip:

Get a copy of the editorial calendar for a newspaper or magazine you're trying to pitch. This is a listing of special sections and topics they have planned throughout the year. Review the calendar and find a specific issue where your topic would be a good fit. Then, call the publication, ask for the name of the person who edits that section and write or E-mail them with your story idea. Do this several months in advance.

Joan Stewart, *The Publicity Hound*

❧

Cost Savings Tip:

Pitching a magazine or newspaper can be a costly endeavor, especially if you're targeting several different publications. Also, you might "think" a magazine or newspaper is right for your market, then after subscribing, you find that it isn't. One way of not having to empty your pocketbook at a newsstand or end up with twenty different subscriptions is to frequent your local library to see what issues they carry. Spend an afternoon researching your publication. If that's not an option for you there are a number of magazine sites that offer free trial issues when you sign up. That way, you can get a look at the magazine and decide whether it's the right publication for your work before you spend the money subscribing. Remember, if you do end up subscribing, keep a note of it for your yearly taxes. Subscriptions are the first thing people forget to write off because they usually aren't accompanied by a receipt.

Don't be afraid to go out on a limb. That's where the fruit is.

❧ H. Jackson Browne

28

C-Span

C-Span offers a myriad of good programs you should consider pitching. Specifically, BookTV and BookNotes are great avenues for authors to get out information on their books. Here's the information for both programs:

BookTV

Since its inception, C-Span's BookTV has covered topics from children's books to history books, political novels to social issues. They also focus on events around the world, live signings, author interviews and publishing world updates. Their programs are cutting edge and very well put together. BookTV has proved to be a great instrument for authors and they welcome ideas, suggestions and innovative ways authors are making a difference in the literary world.

To submit a program idea, contact:

Amy Roach, Producer or
Andrew Murray, Producer
C-Span2 BookTV

400 North Capital Street NW, Suite 650
Washington, DC 20001
(202) 737-3220 phone
(202) 737-0580
Amy's e-mail: aroach@c-span.org
Andrew's e-mail: amurray@c-span.org

Mail a press kit, or contact the producers directly via telephone. If they're interested, they'll contact you.

Booknotes

C-Span's signature author interview program has served as a forum for books about history, politics and public affairs for a dozen years. The unedited, commercial-free format, allows for an in-depth discussion with an author distinct from other author interview programs.

Their format is simple: one author, one book, one hour. For a full hour every Sunday night, fifty-two weeks a year, an author discusses their recently-released book (they consider nonfiction only). Beyond the book's subject matter, authors are also queried about the writing process, about how and why they came to write their book and their own lives and influences. Authors may appear on Booknotes only once in their writing career.

The host of the program since its inception is C-SPAN CEO Brian Lamb. With over 630 author interviews since 1989 consisting of heads of state, war correspondents, biographers, scholars, generals and peacemakers, Lamb's Booknotes provides a variety of perspectives for its viewers. Guests have included Colin Powell, Richard Nixon, Jimmy Carter, Neil Sheehan, Martin Gilbert, Jean Strouse, Betty Friedan, and Henry Louis Gates.

Mail two copies of your book to:

Robin Scullin, Producer
C-Span Booknotes
400 North Capital Street NW, Suite 650
Washington, DC 20001
(202) 737-3220 phone
(202) 737-6226
rscullin@c-span.org

29

The Morning Shows

$\mathcal{E}$very author has at some point nurtured the dream of getting on
a high-profile morning show. How someone goes about doing
this is a whole different matter. The pressure is really on for producers to find stories that are gripping
and visual and not too complicated. Keep
it simple. Bottom line.

Remember that if you're featured on
one show, you probably won't be featured
on another. Unless you're the hottest
story in the country, most morning shows
won't follow their competitors. Now if you

decide to pitch all three shows, you might want to mention that in
your cover letter. That way, there will be no surprises and if your
topic is something they're interested in featuring, they'll get right
back to you to ensure exclusivity.

The Art of the Morning Show Pitch

Pitching any show is truly an art form but morning shows are a
league unto themselves. I never realized this until I was knee-deep

in my own marketing campaign some years ago. I had pitched every angle, every show, and every producer to no avail. No one cared. And why should they? I hadn't refined my story, watched their shows or bothered to tie my story into something newsworthy. I was fortunate enough during that brief period of floundering to have the guidance of a producer who took the time to give me a short but thorough education on the art of the pitch.

She told me to first of all watch her show. Now, while that may seem like an obvious thing to do, most authors who pitch themselves don't really know the demographics of the show they're pitching. For example, if you're pitching something to a national morning show (i.e. *Today Show, Good Morning America, CBS The Early Show*), you'll need to know that the attention span of anyone watching is about twenty minutes. With individual segments running about seven minutes each. It's rare for a viewer to watch a morning show from start to finish. Consequently, what you pitch must be quick and to the point. Leave the investigative reporting to *Dateline* or *48 Hours* when viewers are prepared to sit through thirty-minute segments. Also, if you think sitting there watching you be interviewed is going to enthrall viewers, think again. No one likes a talking head, meaning that if you're pitching something to a show, give the producer some additional material to work from. Video footage, pictures, or whatever it is that can help add some flavor to your segment. While the average demographic will vary slightly from show to show, all of them are vying for the attention of women ages eighteen to forty-nine. If you can send them a bit that targets this specific market, you'll probably have a better chance of getting in the door.

She gave me another significant piece of advice: if your pitch doesn't fit on the back of a business card, you haven't refined it enough. Pitches that are lengthy won't get the attention of a producer. Confine your pitch to a quick, attention grabbing statement. Once you've piqued their interest, you can expand on your idea. Also, offer guests you know you can get in contact with and propose an entire segment rather than just a story idea.

When you're set to pitch your story, be it to a small local station or a major national program, you'll need to remember to do one thing: Think like a producer. It took me a while to grasp that concept. But now, when I'm pitching a client to a show I always ask myself: "Why should they care?" What is it about your segment suggestion that could actually benefit the show? Forget for a moment that you'd like to get on national television and sell a million books. What is it about your topic that will interest their viewers? Ultimately, what's best for the show is all a good producer cares about.

Finally, be excited about your topic. If the topic you're pitching doesn't register with you on some sort of emotional Richter scale, you can bet no one else will care about it either.

Here are the shows and their guidelines:

The Today Show

If you keep up on the morning shows, you know that they've recently added an extra hour to their program. This leaves the field wide open for authors to pitch their ideas. Your book or story idea should be something that people are talking about. If you can tie it in to a hot news story, all the better. This is especially true if your novel is fiction. Because their time is limited, it's tough for them to feature a fictional author unless you're a household name. Sports-related books are generally not featured unless they are newsworthy. One good rule of thumb is not to E-mail your pitch to Andrea Smith; submit your book or galley to her first. Once she has had a chance to peruse it, you can call to follow up.

Andrea Smith, Producer
NBC News Today
30 Rockefeller Plaza, 3rd Floor
NYC, NY 10112

Media Tip:

If you're lucky enough to get on any morning show, don't try to sell your book on the air. Focus on giving a great interview, and who knows, you may get called back someday. Be generous with your information, be helpful, offer solutions. Keep it professional.

❦

Andrea Smith is the best contact for authors. Her numbers are: (212) 664-4371 or 1 (800) NBCNEWS, ext 4371.

Good Morning America

Patty Neger, Senior Segment Producer at GMA says that she likes to see your packet first. Then, wait about three to four days before calling her back and never call her before 1:30 p.m. when the next day's show is in pre-production. The same holds true if you send a fax. Don't call the same day asking if she received it; give her a day or two to read it. Unless your topic ties into a hot story, in which case she'll want to hear from you right away. Patty also says she reads all of her e-mail and does, from time to time, consider pitches that are sent to her that way. One thing GMA will not consider featuring are fictional books.

Patty Neger, Book Editor and Senior Segment Producer
Good Morning America ABC-TV
147 Columbus Avenue, 6th Floor
New York, NY 10023
Her E-mail address is: patty.neger@abc.com
(212) 456-6157 Phone
(212) 456-7290 Fax

Pitching Tip: When pitching your segment, you might try sending a packet to the show's topic-related expert. For example, John Nash is the aviation expert for *Good Morning America*. When you're pitching Patty Neger, you might want to send a copy of your book to John as well.

The Early Show

Carol Story is always on the lookout for new authors and they do not discriminate against self-published authors. While the show does feature both novelists and nonfiction authors, their most popular topics are: personal finance, sports, living & health, general interest, and human interest. Contact her initially by E-mail or US mail. If you're going to call, do so after 11 a.m. and don't call on Friday afternoon. Keep in mind that authors are featured up to five times a week on this show, so this could be a great resource.

Carol Story, Producer
CBS The Early Show
524 W. 57th Street
NYC, NY 10019
cas@cbsnews.com or
theearlyshow@cbsnews.com
(212) 975-4112 Phone
(212) 975-2115 Fax

Do's and Don'ts for Pitching the Morning Shows:

- Never, ever pitch the hosts
- Always, always double check your work for typos. Typographical errors are always a big turn off.
- If you can get guests to enhance your segment, mention that in your cover letter. But don't promise what you can't deliver.

- Unless noted otherwise, don't E-mail your pitch.
- Don't call on the biggest news day of the year unless your book is related to the breaking events.

❧

Did you know?

Many media people have spam filters set up on their e-mail. To avoid getting your message sent straight to the trash bin, watch out for words that trigger spam filters on your recipient's e-mail. Words like "free" or "cash, cash, cash" or "make money fast!" will all trigger these filters and get your message deleted before it's even read. Also, DON'T USE CAPS UNLESS YOU'RE YELLING AT SOMEONE. Besides the fact that it's annoying, caps are also filter triggers.

Don't be afraid to take a big step. You can't cross a chasm
in two small jumps.

✱ David Lloyd George

30

Getting On Oprah

$\mathcal{S}$o you think you're Oprah material, do you? Well, join the crowd. The mere mention of her name sends shivers down my spine. Appearing on the show has turned many unknown authors into tomorrow's superstars. It is the crown jewel, and it must be handled carefully.

Now, if you think that one book and one media kit is all it's going to take to get on her show, I've got news for you. It's been known to take as long as three years, or as short as a week. It all depends on you and what you're pitching, and, it's important to know what has been chosen in the past. A good way to get a feel for this is to visit her web site at www.oprah.com. There, you'll find current and past programs going back as far as 1996.

Oprah is typically interested in books penned by women that often deal with some sort of family issue. Often, they are nonfiction ranging in category from self-help, nutrition, family issues, relationships and everything in between. When pitching for the show, it's important to frequent the web site, watch the show to see what's coming up, where the interests are and what producers might be looking for.

Before you even think about approaching this show, get yourself some local media exposure first. Oprah will rarely feature someone who hasn't done media and there's a rigorous interview process to challenge all of your media skills. They want to be as certain as they can that they're not going to feature someone who will freeze on camera, or not have the kind of media presence the show needs.

One of the best ways to increase your chances of getting on the show is targeting the right people. Here is a very coveted list of the show's producers and their titles. Titles are very important and should be added to any correspondence with the show.

Send a copy of your book and media kit to each of them at the following address:

Harpo Productions
110 North Carpenter
Chicago, IL 60607
(312) 633-0808
Executive Producer: Dianne Atkinson Hudson
Senior Supervising Producers: Alice McGee
    Katy Murphy Davis
    Dana Newton-Utigard
    Ellen Rakietan
Producers:
    Laura Grant Sillars,
    Kandi Amelon
    Jill Barancik
    Lisa Morin
    Jill Von Lokeren-Kuenstler
    Amy Coleman
    Lisa Erspamer
    Angie Kraus
    Jack Mori
    Andrea Wishom

Know that if you send something to Oprah, she might not peruse it herself. She has an army of producers and assistants that weed through the huge amounts of mail and books they receive. Two producers who should be at the top of your list are Alice McGee and Dianne Atkinson Hudson.

So what is the secret for getting on the show? Well, I'll tell you this, it's a better kept secret than Mrs. Field's cookie recipe or the Colonel's secret herbs and spices. But many publicists agree that there are a few guidelines worth following if you're going to even be considered. First, never assume that your book is show-worthy and don't mark your package that way. Just put together a professional media kit, include a copy of your book and send it off. I will reiterate: don't mark the outside with "The Oprah Show": that's the quickest way for your book to land up in never-never land.

One of the things I loved about putting this book together is that it got me in touch with some of the most amazing people. One of them, Pamela Waller (author of *Treasure My Heart*) is part of an E-mail group I belong to. Well, one day she posted a message to all of us stating that she'd gotten a meeting scheduled with Oprah herself. Wow, I thought. How did she do that? When I interviewed her for this book, I was shocked to find the answer was quite simple. "I E-mailed her, I told her who I was and that I'd written a book." She said. That was it. Don't you just love simplicity? "Her assistant contacted me soon after that," Pamela continued, "then, as I understand it, Oprah bought a copy of my book." Can you just hear every single publisher on Madison Avenue cringe at this? People sending boxes of books to hand out, and one simple E-mail gets her time with Oprah. I think that's the beauty of all this marketing we authors do. While you can follow each marketing guide to the letter, or hire the most expensive publicist money can buy, sometimes it's the simplest idea that garners the most attention. Good luck Pamela, we'll all be watching Oprah's book list hoping someday to see you on it.

Remember, above all else, regardless of what the producers say or how fancy your package is, Oprah must love the book. She has said this herself. That perhaps, is the secret to it all.

31

Contacting The Associated Press

Stories written by the Associated Press (the world's largest media organizations) reach over 1,500 daily and weekly newspapers and countless TV and radio stations around the globe. Known for its breaking news coverage, this news service has over 235 bureaus worldwide. You can pitch them like you would any other media contact. The caveat here is that your story MUST have a strong national or international appeal. You can of course pitch your state bureau with state-specific news and they will consider that as well.

The best way to pitch your AP office is via fax. Most offices house only a few employees, making phone pitches too time consuming.

The list below is a smattering of the bureaus around the country. If you don't see one listed for your town, call one of the other offices to see if they can refer you. Or check your local listings.

Bureau Chiefs are listed by each as your primary contact. If no Bureau Chief is listed, call them for the name of their News Editor. Here are the offices around the country:

Los Angeles Bureau:
221 S. Figueroa Street, Suite 300
Los Angeles, CA 90012-2553
(213) 626-1200 phone
(213) 346-0200 fax
Bureau Chief: Sue Cross

Austin Bureau
1005 Congress Avenue, Suite 995
Austin, TX 78701-2469
(512) 472-4004 phone
(512) 469-0800 fax
Bureau Chief: Kelley Shannon

Dallas Bureau
4851 Lyndon B. Johnson Freeway, Suite 300
Dallas, TX 75244-6047
(972) 991-2100 phone
(972) 991-7207 fax
Bureau Chief: John Lumpkin

Denver Bureau
1444 Wazee Street, Suite 130
Denver, CO 80202-1395
(303) 825-0123 phone
(303) 892-5927 fax
Bureau Chief: Peter Mattiace

Houston Bureau
16945 Northcase Drive, Suite 2110
Houston, TX 77060-2151
(281) 872-8900 phone
(281) 872-9988 fax
Bureau Chief: none listed

Las Vegas Bureau
1111 W. Bonanza Road
Las Vegas, NV 89106-3545
(702) 382-7440 phone
(702) 382-0790
News Editor: Tom Tait

Phoenix Bureau
500 N. 3rd Street, Suite 120
Phoenix, AZ 85004-3999
(602) 258-8934
(602) 254-9573 fax
Bureau Chief: Steve Elliott

Portland Bureau
121 SW Salmon Street, Suite 1450
Portland, OR 97204-2924
(503) 228-2169 phone
(503) 228-5514 fax
Bureau Chief: Bryan Brumley

San Diego Bureau
350 Camino De La Reina
San Diego, CA 92108-2098
(619) 231-3587 phone
(619) 291-2098 fax
Bureau Chief: Michelle Morgante

San Francisco Bureau
1390 Market Street, Suite 318
San Francisco, CA 94102-5405
(415) 621-7432 phone
(415) 552-9430 fax
Bureau Chief: Clayton Haswell

San Jose Bureau
675 N. 1st Street, Suite 1170
San Jose, CA 95112-5118
(408) 293-2324 phone
(408) 293-2005 fax
Bureau Chief: none listed

Seattle Bureau
201 Boren Avenue, N
Seattle, WA 98109-5304
(206) 682-1812 phone
(206) 621-1948 fax
Bureau Chief: Dale Leach

Marketing Tip

USA Today is publishing a new E-mail newsletter about
books. A weekly gossip column by Life Editor, Tara
McKelvey will be called "Hot Type." Send her your info via
e-mail to: tmckelvey@usatoday.com

32

Radio, Reaching
For The Masses

*H*ow can you reach millions of people without ever leaving your
home? Why, radio, of course. As our commutes grow longer,
we spend more time in our cars than ever before. We almost live in
a virtual society. We often don't know our neighbor but yet we still
need to feel connected somehow. That's where radio comes in.

There are two types of radio interviews. The first is in-studio,
which means exactly that. You go into the studio and get to meet
with the host directly. The second is called phone-in or "phoners."
This means that you can take the call in your robe and slippers if
you want to, and no one will be the wiser. My recommendation
though; be comfortable, but be prepared. Sometimes making the
call from your home can seem like you're just talking on the
phone to a friend. Keep in mind that you are still speaking to the
masses, even if you are wearing bunny slippers.

I was telling a friend of mine the other day that I was interviewed on a radio station in Hawaii. "Wow," she said, "you got to
go to Hawaii. How exciting!" Well exciting yes, but to tell the truth I
never set foot in Hawaii to do this interview. I sat here in my office,

my feet propped up on the desk talking with a DJ who had graciously agreed to interview me. Most radio stations use "phoners" and most guests love appearing on radio this way. Did you know that there are more than 1,400 radio talk shows that need guests on a constant basis? If you're willing to do your research, I guarantee there's a radio show with your name on it.

There are a lot of pros and cons about radio interviews. First of all, you're probably going to get more time on radio than you would on television. And, while television is visual, when you're on radio you'll get a better chance to expand on your subject matter and get across exactly what you want to say. If you live in the city

where the interview takes place, then I recommend that you go to the studio if at all possible.

When you position yourself for radio, I suggest going for the larger cities. Now, this doesn't mean turning down smaller stations. As a matter of fact, unless you feel the program or radio demographic is not in your best interest, I wouldn't turn down any offer to speak on radio. Every time you get to do a program, you are honing your skills. You get better every time, and with luck, by the time you hit a huge demographic—you'll be an absolute pro.

Now, when pitching yourself for radio keep one thing in mind. You're the expert and you're providing a solution. If you can solve people's problems, they will love you. If your book provides a solution, great! If it doesn't, then find the story or the controversy behind the book, or promote the story behind the author. The book, at this point, might even become secondary. Keep that in mind when you're pitching the stations. While your book might not be of particular interest to the show's producer, how you sell it must be. When I was trying to garner media attention for *The Cliffhanger*, I realized that romantic fiction might not get me on the airwaves, but the publishing story surrounding it could. So I began to develop a plan, a well-thought-out promotional campaign based on the method of publishing (the new on-line publishers) as opposed to the book itself. The book at that point became less of a statement and more of an example of what discouraged authors can do to promote themselves. It worked! There was a huge amount of interest in this particular subject, and while I still sold my books, it was more out of curiosity for the product rather than its content.

When you are speaking on the air, don't sound too canned. And don't sound like a politician. Rehearsed speeches will come over just that way. And most of us don't have the proper training to take a rehearsed speech and make it sound natural. Know your stuff and speak like the authority you are. Always remember: you're there to share your message, offer a solution and sell your book.

One of the best pieces of advice someone ever gave me was "Be enthusiastic!" If you're not excited about your product or your message, how can you expect your listener to be? Also, make a list of a few points you want to make and keep making them through your talk. Keep in mind that if you're recording this in advance, some of what you say will get edited out so you want to make your most vital statements enough so that they have a chance to be heard. It might not even be a bad idea to have a mission statement or index cards with your points listed on them so you can keep referring back to them throughout your interview.

Now, of course, even though your book might be secondary as we discussed above, you still want to get people interested in it. How about creating a highlight sheet or tip sheet from your talk and faxing it to anyone who calls in to request it? That way you can include your book's information on the sheet as well. If they like your tip sheet, they'll most likely order the book.

So, now that you're ready for radio… how to get on the air? Well, a good place to start is Radiospace.com. This site will link you to radio shows and stations across the country. It's a great resource if you're pitching an idea and can't figure out where to go. Click on Programming Resources, this will take you directly to their list of stations and syndicated programs.

"See" you on the airwaves!

Radio Tip:

Don't forget! Bring a cassette tape to the studio or send one in advance if you're going to be a "phoner." This really came in handy for me when I was doing an in studio spot during a book tour in Oregon. It was a small station and they did not record any of their programming. Thankfully, I was able to whip out my tape and I had a copy of the show. Good thing because it turned out to be a great program.

⋆

Tips for a Successful Radio Interview:

From *Jump Start Your Book Sales* by Marilyn & Tom Ross— Available at your local bookstore or by calling (800) 331-8355 or at www.spannet.org/cc.

- Assume that you're on the air as soon as you pick up the phone. This probably won't be the case but you never know when you're comments will be recorded.
- Try to listen to the station and the show you're going to be on ahead of time. You can often do this from their site on the Web but if nothing else, you can always call the station during the program and ask to be put on hold.
- Stand up when you speak. Sitting will cause you to slouch so get out your cordless phone and walk around. You'll sound more dynamic that way.
- Remember that radio producers and hosts do talk to one another. There are sites on the Web where they can

discuss their guests. Be a great guest and you might get calls from stations you didn't even pitch.

- Always put your best voice forward and remember that you are auditioning from the moment you begin to speak. Think that producer is calling to check a detail? Maybe. But more than likely, he's calling to hear your voice inflection and your level of enthusiasm. So turn on the charm.

Make Every Interview Count

If you're able to get the radio or television interview, make sure to tape it or get a copy. Armed with that, you can now get the interview digitized (transferred to CD). Once it's transferred, it's a lot easier to include a CD in your press kit than a bulky tape. If you have a computer with a CD burner all the better. You can burn your own CD's, make labels for them and you've got another great looking piece of marketing material to include with your media kits. Not only that, but you can also attach a digitized copy of your interview to the press room on your web site. That way people can go on-line and see your interview as well.

33

National Public Radio

$\mathcal{F}$rom my perspective, National Public Radio (NPR) is a gold mine. If you've spent any time listening to their broadcasts (and I highly encourage you to do this), you'll note that they not only offer very thorough reporting, but also give their audience a very wide variety of programs from which to choose. From *Car Talk* to *Talk of the Nation*, the possibilities are endless. At last report, they had a listener base of 19.3 million with 600 affiliate stations nationwide.

Before you pitch anyone on the list below, listen to their program. As with anything, you'll want to cater your pitch. Once you've determined who you want to contact, send them a copy of your book with a pitch letter detailing why this book would be perfect featured on their show. If you're pitching an issue, it's always an added bonus if you can pitch something that was featured on their program (as a follow-up topic) or something that might be a current news story.

As with any medium, their shows need lead-time so send them an advanced copy whenever possible. And keep in mind that some of the NPR folks will not feature someone who has already been interviewed on another show. When you're pitching, send your media kit to as many as you feel are appropriate to your topic but know that once it's been featured, that's probably it for a while. Once, however, may be all you need.

Morning Edition

Ellen McDonnell, Executive Producer
Jim Wallace, Producer
635 Massachusetts Avenue, NW
Washington, DC 20001
(202) 414-2000 Phone
(202) 414-3329 Fax
Jwallace@npr.org
Emcdonnell@npr.org

Show format: While you sleep the world makes news. And the staff of Morning Edition is working "round-the-clock" to keep you up to date. Tune in Friday to *Morning Edition* with Bob Edwards from NPR News. They feature: current events, business, sports, and history. Four ten minute segments each day.

Pitching advice: One sure-fire way to get blacklisted is to leave Jim a voice mail message. You can E-mail him your pitch initially, then follow up to see if there's an interest. You might go ahead and tell him in your E-mail that you're going to send him a book and media kit. It's rare that Jim will feature a book on his show. More often than not, their guests are issue related.

All Things Considered

Carol Klinger, Editorial Assistant
635 Massachusetts Avenue, NW
Washington, DC 20001
(202) 414-2107 Phone
(202) 414-3329 Fax

Show format: Arts, history, science, biography, fiction and everything in-between.

Pitching advice: Try not to pitch by phone. If you must call, do so before 10 a.m. or after 4 p.m. Pitch by mail initially, then call to follow-up. She also loves to hear about emerging authors, so get your story to her.

Alan Cheuse, Book Critic
MS IC3
George Mason University
Fairfax, VA 22030
(703) 993-1183 Phone
(703) 993-1161 Fax

Pitching advice: Alan's reviews are featured on *All Things Considered.* His reviews run two to three minutes two times per week on the show. He will review literary fiction and genre books (mystery, sci-fi).

Weekend, All Things Considered
Fred Wasser, Associate Producer/Director
635 Massachusetts Avenue, NW
Washington, DC 20001
(202) 414-2144 Phone
(202) 414-3029 Fax
fwasser@npr.org

Show format: This show will feature one or two authors and airs Saturday and Sunday. Much like *All Things Considered,* anything goes.

Pitching advice: Fred must see your book so don't send your media kit without it. Give him a chance to peruse it, then call to check and see if he's received it. Or, you can E-mail him initially; follow up with your press kit and then call.

Talk of the Nation
Ellen Silva, Producer
635 Massachusetts Avenue, NW
Washington, DC 20001
(202) 513-2342 Phone
(202) 414-3029 Fax

Show format: This show is syndicated in Europe and runs eight times per week. They feature at least one author every day. If you've listened to their show, you know their topics tend to vary a great deal. Generally though, they are topical and public affairs related. They run The Book Club the second to last Thursday of every month. They like diversity in their authors and begin announcing future guests four months in advance. See what I mean about advance copies?

Pitching advice: Even though I stress advance copies, try not to send your media kit naked. She usually won't consider something that is fresh of the press unless it's already garnered a heap of buzz. Include some reviews and press clippings with your packet.

The Tavis Smiley Show
JJ Southerland, Producer
4434 Crenshaw Blvd.
Los Angeles, CA 90043
(323) 290-4690
jjsoutherland@npr.org

Show Format: Host Tavis Smiley's trademark passion and energy fuel the show, which features substantive and provocative discussions, commentary, and reports on everything from politics to pop culture. An insightful exploration of the issues that matter from fresh, diverse point of views is the show's hallmark.

The Tavis Smiley Show will feature regular guests including Michael Eric Dyson, a religion professor from DePaul University;

technology guru Omar Wasow, the executive director of blackplanet.com; UCLA law professor Kimberly Crenshaw; and Harvard University's Cornel West and Charles Ogletree, professors of religion and law, respectively. On Fridays the show will take a lighter tone, with guests such as comedians Paul Mooney and Cheryl Underwood, offering humorous takes on current events.

Time selected Smiley as one of America's 50 most promising young leaders. Newsweek profiled him as one of the "20 people changing how Americans get their news" and dubbed him one of the nation's "captains of the airwaves." The *New York Post* shouted "Look out Larry King—here comes Tavis Smiley!"

Fresh Air
Amy Salit, Producer
150 N. Sixth Street
Philadelphia, PA 19106
(215) 351-1242 Phone
(215) 592-7012 Fax
asalit@whyy.org

Show format: Typically, Amy is open to any topic and won't rule out anything initially. Interviews on this show can run as long as an hour. Pitch yourself, not the book.

Pitching advice: Amy likes a lot of information. Don't forget to include your resume, any news clippings and previous interviews if you have them digitized.

Maureen Corrigan, Book Critic
Georgetown University
C/o Department of English
New North Building, Room 309
Washington, DC 20057
(202) 687-7431

Show format: Maureen is the reviewer for *Fresh Air*. She will review one book per week. She will consider both fiction as well as nonfiction and loves biography, memoirs and history. Don't fret though, she's been known to review the not-so-serious books as well, so send her your fun summer read too.

Weekend Edition, Saturday

Julia Bailey, Producer
Sean Collins, Producer
635 Massachusetts Avenue, NW
Washington, DC 20001
(202) 414-2274
jbailey@npr.org
scollins@npr.org

Show format: The show's host, Scott Simon, likes pop-culture and enlightening nonfiction. He's also interested in anything on Chicago, Quakerism, baseball and spirituality. Anything that is unusual will pique his curiosity as well. A portion of the show is news related but they also cover some very bizarre issues as well.

Pitching advice: I pitched Julia initially and told her (briefly) what my topic was, then I closed by informing her that I would be sending a book and media kit. She told me that she appreciated me doing that. And while my package still got lost, the E-mail did not. She files them in certain folders within her E-mail program and keeps them for an undetermined amount of time.

Weekend Edition, Sunday

Neil Carruth, Assistant Editor
635 Massachusetts Avenue, NW
Washington, DC 20001
(202) 513-2885
ncarruth@npr.org

Show format: This show goes after the unusual. Most of their topics are serious but occasionally they will go after a funny segment. They feature books in the second half of their show. Neil is new to this program so this format might be changing.

Pitching advice: Send him an E-mail pitch first, then follow up to see if there's an interest before you send him more material. Depending on the subject matter and segment, he might have specific items he will need to see before making his decision.

Public Interest
Diane Vogel, Executive Producer
WAMU-FM
4000 Brandywine Street, NW
Washington, DC 20016
(202) 885-1226
dvogel@wamu.org
John Haas, Producer
Terry Cross-Davis, Producer
jhaas@wamu.org
tcrossdavis@wamu.org

Show format: Call-in radio show with host Kojo Nnamdi, tackles politics, science, popular culture, social issues, and more. Produced by WAMU in Washington, DC. Special features include the Computer Guys, the popular monthly program on computers, software, and issues in cyberspace. They are looking for new and exciting authors and will put panels together if the topic warrants.

Pitching advice: Send your books to Elaine. If you want to leave a message, contact Graham.

Diane Rehm
Elizabeth Terry, Producer
WAMU-FM
4000 Brandywine Street, NW

Washington, DC 20016
(202) 885-1228

Show format: A public affairs and call-in program analyzes the news and examines issues that affect our daily lives. Produced by WAMU in Washington, DC, guests range from Archbishop Desmond Tutu and Gloria Steinem, to John Updike and Maya Angelou.

Pitching advice: They like to interview authors right when your book comes out. Diane Rehm likes to do the first interview and won't follow *Talk of the Nation* or *Public Interest*. They will consider an author who's been on *Fresh Air*. Elizabeth says to send your book, she'll call

Living on Earth
Jennifer Chu, Producer—Book segments
8 Story Street
Cambridge, MA 02138
(617) 868-8810 phone
(617) 868-8659 fax
chuniser@loe.org

Show format: If you have an environment-related issue this show is for you. The multi-award winning program with host Steve Curwood, explores our environment, what we're doing to it, and what it's doing to us. In-depth coverage, features, interviews, and commentary examine how the environment affects medicine, politics, technology, economics, transportation, agriculture, and more.

Bookworm
KCRW-FM
1900 Pico Blvd.
Santa Monica, CA, 90405

Show Format: Bookworm is an exciting new program on KCRW (NPR affiliate). The station is based in Santa Monica and welcomes in-studio guests only at this time. If you're going to be in the LA area, this is a great program to consider. You'll want to first check out their web site at kcrw.org to make sure your book is a match for their programming. They focus on literary fiction and poetry. Occasionally they will also consider literary nonfiction.

Pitching advice: To submit books for consideration, send a copy of the book, at least one month before the author will be coming to Los Angeles. Do not follow-up on your submission. If the host, Michael Silverblatt, is interested, he will get back to you. If he likes something, he gets right on it. No news is not good news.

34

Verify Everything!

The quickest way to have your press release or media kit hit the circular file is to have it addressed to someone who left to go to the competitor. I've noticed that often names I had for media contacts as little as two months ago might no longer be good, so double check everything. It only takes a quick phone call and you can rest assured that your packet or press release will end up in the right hands, instead of someone's trash can.

35

Tenacity Should Be Your Middle Name

I say, keep following up until you get a "no." And even then, wait an appropriate length of time, maybe a few months, and then try pitching again. If you get a "it's wrong for our format" then move on, but if the response is "not right now, but maybe in the future" that's your key to stay in touch.

Wait about two weeks, then make three or more follow-up calls; more for bigger media targets. What doesn't interest the media today, might interest them tomorrow or maybe even next year. Stay in front of them, keep sending newsworthy press releases. Send your postcards; whatever it takes. Be persistent but don't be obnoxious. Jenice Gharib, Editor of *Vision Magazine*, suggests that following up should be an art rather than a science, "I think it is really important to develop an ongoing relationship with an editor. Prior to your book release and after it. Especially with local magazines, papers, or trade journals. Editors are more inclined to review or write about books and authors they know.

That doesn't mean the 'out of the blue' book won't get in. It just gives them a better chance."

Putting Together Your Script

Personally, I've never written a script when I call the media. I think it sounds too canned. What I do, however, is make up a list of points or highlights I want to make sure to mention. Also, it's important for me to know exactly why I'm calling. Or what I wish to accomplish with my call. If you do get someone on the phone and don't end up in voice mail, knowing what your purpose is will help direct the call exactly where you want it to go. When you're determining this, be specific. It's Murphy's law that if you're not specific, you'll just end up getting "whatever". You don't want "whatever," you want something much more specific than that, don't you? Finally, if you don't sound crisp and directed, the person on the other end will become disinterested very quickly.

Following Up

Your follow-up process should start about two weeks after you've sent your media kit and book. If you actually get to talk to the person you're pitching and don't land up in voice mail, you might think about starting your conversation with: "Is this a good time?" or "Are you on a deadline?" This shows that you understand that they are busy. You are respectful of their time and you're beginning to win them over. Next, be concise in your statement, whether you're speaking to someone live or on voice mail. A trick I learned years ago as a telephone operator was to smile when you talk. It's a good thing to remember because your smile comes across on the telephone. Whatever you do, don't let any sense of impatience you might feel bleed through to your conversation. The person on the other end will pick up on that. It must sound like you're calling them for the first time, not the hundredth. Also, when you're checking

Would You Believe?

Some people who are asked to call back by the media are sometimes never heard from again. Could you imagine, getting permission to call back, then blowing it off? Hmmm.

back, try to sound excited about what you're pitching. This might not be so difficult in the beginning but after several contacts you might begin to feel the doldrums setting in. If that's the case, put off calling for another day or go outside for a walk, do whatever you have to to empower yourself to make those calls.

Postcards

Before I send a media kit, I will send a postcard announcing its arrival. Once the media kit is sent, I wait about three days and send another one asking the simple question: "Have you seen your media kit yet?" Now, the person receiving this card might not really care whether they've seen this particular media kit but when they do come across it they'll recognize the front cover. This recognition might be all it takes to get your media kit to float to the top of the slush pile. I also use these same postcards to send quick notes, thank you's or whatever else strikes my fancy. For example you probably all remember the Presidential election of 2000, right? Well it took place during the time I was marketing my first book, *The Cliffhanger*. All through the ups and downs of counting chads (both dimpled and non-dimpled) they kept referring to this election as a "cliffhanger"—I knew that I would have to hang up my marketing hat if I could not take full advantage of this play on words. In a flash it came to me. I sent out 400 postcards with the following slogan on the back:

Getting tired of the Presidential cliffhanger?
Try this one.
The Cliffhanger, a novel.
No politics involved.

Did I have these postcards printed especially for this? No way. Knowing that the election could get called at any moment, I was frantic to get these out. So, I went to my local office supply store and purchased clear labels. I typed in the text I wanted, printed them on my printer, adhered them to the postcards and sent them off. Out of the entire mailing, only one person responded. It was a local TV anchor who loved the tie-in and held up my post card during their morning show. He read the back of it then proceeded to tell everyone watching to go out and buy my book. *The Cliffhanger* shot up to the #1 best selling book in San Diego where it remained for three months. It only takes one mention. And those who didn't respond were, at the very least, reminded of my book one more time. Repetition is important. If someone you've been pitching sees your book enough, they'll think it's probably worth a call back.

Getting Into Voice Mail

A good trick to try when leaving voice mails is to hit the # key after you've left the message. Now this might be different for every voice mail system, but unless you get instruction prior to leaving your message, it's a good safe bet that by pressing the number sign you'll be able to review your message. I do this all the time and if I find that I've said "uh" too much, I delete the message and start over. I've been told that more often than not, voice mail is used as a way to screen the story initially. With that in mind, you'll want to sound as upbeat and as excited as you can. I once left a voice mail message for *The Today Show* so full of excitement, they called me back less than forty-eight hours later (which is an incredible turnaround time). Sure, I had left several messages prior and gotten no response. Finally, I decided to reinvent my idea and add an octave or two of power to my script.

When you're trying to garner media attention, try to angle your pitch to something that's already happening in the news. If it's news-related, contact them right away. Don't wait on this. If you have something related to a breaking story, this could be your chance. No one will care about it in 24 or 48 hours.

Always, always, always reference the name of your book. No one is going to know you just by your name unless it's John Grisham. Don't say something like: "Did you get my book?" They undoubtedly did but it's stacked in the pile of one hundred books they still have to go through. Be specific. Remember, yours is not the only must-read novel they've got to consider.

Getting Rejected

Remember the time you got your first rejection letter from a publisher? I sure do. I was devastated and crushed that they refused me. Then when the second and third letter came, the feeling began to wane. Make no mistake, it still hurt. But my pride no longer took such a hefty beating with each new "no". Working with the media is the same thing. A "no" today, does necessarily mean a "no" tomorrow. Just like when you were trying to sell your manuscript, it's important to learn from every rejection. What about it made them not want to run your story? Not enough research to back up your topic? Not enough information, or was it too much? If you can, ask before you hang up the phone. It's important to know before you move on to your next conquest. Most of the time you'll find that it's not about you. It might be more about them than anything else. Or perhaps the show you're interested in has changed direction, or maybe someone else with a better pitch beat you to the punch. Find out, file it away in your "what not to do

Rule Of Seven

The Rule of Seven has been taught in business schools for years. Your average prospect needs to be exposed to your book, pitch or sales message at least seven times in eighteen months before they will become a motivated buyer.

❧

next time" folder and move on. There are hundreds more places for you to sell your story.

Remember: You need the press more than they need you!

36

Web Sites

A Few Simple Things You Can Do To Make A Difference

Now that your book is in production, you're going to want to work on your web site. A web site is a constant 24/7 way of promoting you and your book. Make it concise, make it easy to navigate and easy to load, and if possible, get a short web site address. Not only will it be easy for people to remember but if it's too long, you stand the chance of visitors hitting the wrong keys and ending up somewhere other than your site. Some authors put a site together based on the title of their book. Chris Lear, for example, has a site with a similar title to his book, *Running with the Buffaloes*. His web site? www.runwiththebuffs.com. Pretty simple to remember, isn't it? For me, it was simple www.nomorerejections.com as well as my original site www.booksbypen.com. The two are linked so one address will take you to the other and vice versa. If a domain name has got you stumped, try going to nameboy.com. Then, type in your key words, or subject matter and it will generate a list of spiffy names from which to choose.

Make sure to include enough content to make your site interesting and even some stuff that's not directly related to your book.

Give people a reason to return to your site. By giving them fresh, interesting and often updated content, you give them a reason to check back. It's not recommended that you offer tons of information, but if you do, make sure to update it frequently. Keep it current information and fun links. Do this and you'll end up bookmarked for sure.

Listing Your Site

There are a number of ways you can list your web site with search engines. You can pay a service to do this for you, you can do a mass submitting yourself or you can list your site individually at each search engine. Now, while this is the more tedious of the processes, it might be worth your while to consider it. Remember if you make one mistake when mass submitting your site, it could take months to correct it. So let's take a look for a moment at mass submitting and individual submitting.

* **Mass submitting**

Mass submitting is when you access hundreds of on-line search engines through a promotion site (like addme.com, for example). This promotion site will take you through the steps of submitting once you have completed their application form. Be wary of this. While it worked for my site, it also submitted my link to FFA's (Free For All's) and I ended up getting on about four hundred mailing lists. Read the fine print of your agreement with these promotion sites. Most of them are free and a great time saver, but they can cost you in other ways.

- Promotionworld.com—will mass submit your site to over thirty search engines
- Register it! http://register-it.netscape.com/O=wsg/—while this site only submits your link to twelve search engines, their web site garage offers a lot of tools to help with

tracking your site, checking hits per day and other neat stuff to keep your traffic high

- Add Me (www.addme.com) has a myriad of free services to help you drive more traffic to your site.
- Submit2.com—this site will submit to over three hundred search engines, they used to be free but now, I believe, there's a minimal cost for this submission.
- Submit-it.com—they used to be free, now they've got some pretty elaborate packages to choose from.

✎ Individual Submissions

When you opt to submit your site to individual search engines, you are essentially hand submitting to all these sites yourself. Now, while this may seem like a lot of work (it is) it could be well worth your while. You can focus on submitting to the most popular sites (listed below), and then add sites as you come across them or as you feel they are relevant.

✎ Popular Search Engines

- Google
- Alta Vista
- HotBot
- Lycos
- Webcrawler

✎ A Final Note on Site Submissions

If the whole "key word" thing has got you more confused than ever, try heading on over to wordtracker.com or goodkeywords. com. Both of these sites will help dispel the myths of keywords and get you a list of words that will help push your site higher up on the search engine ranking system.

Help Others And You Help Yourself

Wayne Perkins, author of *Three Book Marketing Techniques for the Timid*, offered a great suggestion to me recently. He advised checking into some of the highest-ranking sites in your particular category. Say for example, your topic is childcare. Take a few minutes and search the top ranking sites at Yahoo. Once you generate that list, see if they have their own bookstore (most high-ranking sites do). Click through on one of their book titles and see where it takes you. Say for instance you land up at Amazon. Now take a look at the address in your browser. It probably looks something like this:

http://www.amazon.com/exec/obidos/ASIN/0759638241/

The two most significant parts to this are the ISBN number, which Amazon will list as an ASIN number (their code for ISBN) and the words "kidscare" which is Amazon's way of tracking an affiliate sales member. To get this link ready for your book, you'll want to shave off the number at the end so that the link looks more like this:

http://www.amazon.com/exec/obidos/ASIN/0759638241/kidscare

Now, replace the number after "ASIN" with your book's ISBN number. Take this revised URL and send a quick E-mail to the site's webmaster. Ask him if he'd be willing to feature your book on their site, mention that you've included the sites identifier so that they can continue to generate commissions through Amazon's affiliate program, and include a brief book description and why it would be helpful to their visitors. This is a real win-win situation. Not only will they continue to earn affiliate dollars, but the sales of your book will increase substantially by the exposure generated from such a high-traffic site.

Things No Good Web Site Can Be Without

* **Contact Information**

Don't forget to list your contact information on the home page at your site. According to Joan Stewart, *The Publicity Hound*, this is often overlooked. "If you have a web site, place the author's photo and updated contact information on the home page. Sometimes when trying to contact an author, I go to their web site and then search in desperation for contact info."

* **Press Room**

Eventually, your web site will replace your media kit. All book promotions will be done via E-mail and brochures will be non-existent. Get a head start on this emerging trend by adding a press room to your web site. This will be your virtual media kit. Include any author interviews (digitized copies attached to your page) or real media samples of radio interviews. Make this page fun, informative and interactive. Give whoever is perusing this a reason to stay for a while, a reason to return and a reason to book you on their next show.

* **Who's Watching You?**

Is it a popularity contest? It might be. Check out linkpopularity. com to see how your site ranks in the grand scheme of things!

* **Linking and Affiliate Programs**

If you've never been a part of an affiliate program, here's how it works. You sign up for it, and place a button "click through" link anywhere on your site. Then, if someone clicks on it and makes a purchase you get 4% or whatever the going rate is for that particular site. I have several on my web site and I love them. I even do all my purchases that way instead of going directly to the site. I get paid for my own purchases. I also encourage my friends to shop that way too. It doesn't cost them a thing and you get paid each time they make a purchase. One of the best places I found to get started with affiliate programs is www.linkshare.com. You sign up for an account and pick from literally hundreds upon hundreds of on-line stores. Commission Junction (www.cj.com) is yet another. Peruse both of these sites and see which one offers the stores you think work best with the audience visiting your web site. Sometimes there's an approval process; sometimes not. In any event you copy the HTML text into your site, or have someone do it for you if you're not familiar with site design, and voila. Now, you're a store.

✶ Signatures

Don't forget to add a signature to every single E-mail you send out or respond to. Include your name, your book title and your web site (don't forget to include the http:// before the "www" so people can quickly and easily click directly through to your site). It's another means to advertise and best of all, it's free.

Example:

Penny C. Sansevieri
No More Rejections.
Get Published Today!
Visit our web site at:
http://www.nomorerejections.com

＊ William Feather

37

Creating The Buzz

About a year before they opened, I began hearing that Krispy Kreme had selected our fine city to open up its first shop in the area. None of us living in Southern California had ever eaten one of their donuts. Except maybe those lucky enough to travel back east where these shops are everywhere. But from what I heard, they were amazing. When the Krispy Kreme shop finally opened in my area, you could expect to wait nearly two hours for your own Krispy Kreme goodie. Well, my girlfriends and I simply could no longer resist. So we stood among hundreds of others waiting patiently for our first taste of a real Krispy Kreme donut. Television cameras were everywhere, radio stations were broadcasting from their rooftops, it was amazing. Finally, we had our box. Sitting on a bench we each tried one and guess what. They were donuts. Okay, they were good. But still, they were donuts. All of this commotion, and all over a donut. Amazing when you think about it, isn't it? That's a buzz. It doesn't matter if it's a cure for cancer or a new donut shop. A buzz is a buzz in whatever form. It drives the public attention. Remember when Titanic came out? The buzz on that movie started about two years prior to its release. Often times, a buzz can be overrated as was feared in this case. No one thought it could actually live up the "buzz," but it did. A buzz will generate media interest and thus public interest and even after its launched, it can survive for a long time just on buzz alone.

I spoke to a publisher who told me once that often, most literary houses won't even consider a manuscript if it arrives "sans" buzz. So how do you go about creating a buzz on something that hasn't even hit the streets yet? Well, you could do what Richard Paul Evans, the author of *The Christmas Box*, did. Even though it wasn't published traditionally, he still wanted people to read his book. So he printed off copies, had them bound at his local copy shop and gave them away to everyone he knew. The book was so good that eventually, it started a buzz. He had people calling him he didn't even know asking for a copy of his book. He sold many thousands of copies in the Salt Lake City area alone. Needless to say, he did eventually get it published. And by the time it arrived at the publisher it was loaded with buzz. So much so that the major publishers became interested in the book and dozens of them participated in a two-day auction. Simon & Schuster came out the winner. They only had to pay Evans a $4.2 million advance. The book has sold more than 7,000,000 copies in 17 different languages.

That's the beauty of on-line publishing. You can publish your book, get it out there and start creating such an interest about it that the buzz naturally follows. Eventually, the media will pick up on this and then, if you're lucky, a publisher will stand up and take notice. Now, this, of course, is no guarantee that you'll get picked up traditionally. But more often than not, if a publisher sees that you've got something big, they're going to want a part of it.

Start marketing your book early. So what if it won't be available for another few months. Scarcity often creates demand. If you can garner a few excellent advanced reviews you're almost buzz-assured. Start talking up your book everywhere you go. Get postcards printed up early, get bookmarks made early. Distribute some press releases early on, letting the media know it's coming. Repetition is the key here.

In this book we have been discussing a variety of marketing ideas and strategies. Consider starting them early. Start sending out media kits, start talking it up to people, especially if your topic is timely or can tie into a certain news item. Don't wait! Let the media determine if they can use your story in advance of your book. You want people to start talking about your book. Then, once they're talking, you have to keep the discussion going. I'd like to tell you that keeping this discussion going is easy, but it isn't. A good, but somewhat time consuming way to start people talking about your book is to initiate an on-line discussion about it. Again, this works best if it's a nonfiction genre or a hot topic. Places like talkcity.com or about.com host hundreds of topic discussions. Begin by creating your own community or starting your own topic. You can begin to generate interest about your book.

Another way to find an audience is through newsgroups, chatrooms and E-mail discussions. You will need to find specific chats and E-mail discussion lists that attract the audience you're looking for. You can find chatrooms and E-mail discussion lists by doing a search at Yahoo, Altavista, Excite or Google for starters. Sometimes you can even purchase a list to start a target E-mail campaign, direct sales or newsletter blurbs. Some places will offer these services for free. Coollist.com for example or egroups.com are both great examples of where you can start your own E-mail discussion list for free. You can invite people to join. Often what I'll do is get a sign-up sheet going at a book signing and invite those people to join this discussion group. It's amazing how quickly it will grow. One person tells another and so on. Keep your E-mail discussion groups lively and interesting, give them a reason to become a member and stay a member.

Another good site to check out is bookpromotion.com. They have several packages (beginning at $99) to help you start your book promotion. Copywriter.com is another great on-line business resource center, giving out valuable information about direct E-mail lists, e-zines, newsletters, sponsorable discussion lists and more.

Foxcontent.com is a content-linking site for authors. They claim to be able to create an electronic word-of-mouth. This is not a free service, but the last time I checked their site was down for renovations and I wasn't able to get a cost associated with this service.

Newsgroup/E-mail Discussion Sites

- Groups.google.com (formerly deja.com)
- Tile.net

Marketing Tip

Marketing on a budget? Aren't we all.

If your book is of the right genre, try getting a listing on giftcrap.com.

They offer free placement in their strange, eclectic on-line catalog. To qualify you need a web site where people can purchase your book or a current listing on Amazon.com. Check out their site first to see if your book qualifies.

According to most studies, people's number one fear is public speaking. Number two is death. Death is number two! Does that seem right? That means to the average person if you have to go to a funeral, you're better off in the casket than doing the eulogy.

⚹ Anonymous

38

Speak Up!

*A*uthors ask me all the time: How can I get some recognition for my book? I tell them, speak up! Talk it up, whenever and wherever you can. Public speaking is powerful to not only spread the word about your book but build your credibility on your particular topic.

The thing is, when you first become a published author, people will automatically assume you know everything about your topic (which you should). They also assume you know everything there is to know about the publishing industry as well. I'll be the first one to admit I don't know everything there is to know about the publishing world. Half the fun of it is learning something new every day. But what I do know, I can impart on others and so can you. My first book, *The Cliffhanger*, was fiction, so the emphasis wasn't so much on the book, but on the process of publishing. Now, if you wrote a nonfiction book you can certainly speak about the topic itself. If your book is a historical romance, or a murder mystery there are a

223

number of spins your talk can take. It's not that dissimilar from pitching the media really. The thing is, in this instance, you're pitching for a speaking engagement. Most of the time, you'll be speaking for free. But don't let that discourage you. You can still sell your book, not to mention gaining valuable speaking experience. If the thought of getting up in front of a crowd of people makes you more nervous than a turkey the week before Thanksgiving, know that if you can overcome your fear, public speaking is a powerful tool to get the word out about you and your book.

Most people think that when they sign up to speak publicly they have to develop a persona or gimmick. I say, be yourself. Script what you're going to say, then toss the script and work from 3 x 5 cards so you'll sound more natural and not just a talking head. Go to a Toastmaster's class a few times and get some pointers from the pros. I did this once and was amazed at how many times I said "uh". Uh, get the picture?

There are many, many topics you can speak on and even more places to do just that. Your local Chamber of Commerce is always looking for speakers. How about an organization relating to your topic? There are hundreds of them out there. Check your city's upcoming events calendar. If you pick an event related to your topic with a date that's eight to twelve months out, they are probably still in need of speakers and there might be a spot open with your name on it.

Bragging Rights

Like becoming a new parent or grandparent, you too have bragging rights. So when someone asks you what you do, what exactly do you tell them? I used to say: "Well, I'm an assistant and I like to write." Then, I started telling people I was a writer. That worked for a while, they would usually respond with: "Oooh, that's neat! What kind of books do you write?" But soon, I found that got old too. It was interesting for a while, but as soon as they'd ask me if I'd been on Oprah (usually their second question) I would sheepishly reply that I had not and immediately their attention would wane. Gosh, I used to hate that. Now, when someone asks me what I do for a living I tell them: "I teach people how to break through old barriers and get published." That one line seems to bring with it a plethora of questions, fortunately none of them relating to whether or not I've been on Oprah. Sure, it's bragging. But after persisting through enough rejection letters to wallpaper my apartment, I think I've earned it.

So now, what are you going to tell people when they ask what you do? What one line can you come up with that will intrigue them and get to ask more, and possibly, even buy your book. Think about it. Did you perhaps write a story about a girl who gets herself out of an abusive relationship? How about telling people you are an expert on women who get themselves into and out of abusive relationships. No doubt you did a mountain of research for your book so you probably know what you're talking about, and if you're doing the talk circuit thing you're probably knee deep in statistics, and crisis centers.

When you reach out to people like this, it's not always about you. Sure, it starts out that way. But when you tell someone you're the expert on such and such topic, I guarantee you they'll know someone who could benefit or know someone who knows someone. You might even be in a position to help someone who's lost all hope, and wouldn't that be great? It doesn't always have to be the kind of assistance that will get you the Medal of Honor or a float in the Rose Parade. It could be something as simple as empowering another human being to live their dream and get that book published. Who knows, while you're standing in line at the post office telling the person in front of you that you're a published author and urging them to do the same, you might be talking to the next Andre Dubus.

39

Book Signings

One of the scariest moments in my life was my first book signing. Even more frightening than having my first signing was
the fact that I was doing it out of town and wouldn't have my support group of friends to stop by and play
the role of excited fans. So, I had done
everything by the book. First, I sent
some advance copies of the book to
the store owner, I mailed him the
book cover posters, I made up bag
stuffers and sent the proper press releases to local media. To my chagrin
when I arrived there, the box containing my marketing materials was still
sealed. Not one poster was out, not one bag
stuffer had been used. Worst of all, it poured rain that day. So
there I sat, my dreams of crowds lining up outside the little shop
vanished with each passing second. When one person did show
up, I nearly jumped out of my chair to embrace them. But don't
worry, I somehow managed to contain myself. About an hour after the book signing started, I noticed several people in the store,

none of them paying attention to me. So, I got up and began to walk around the store. I carried my book with me and each time I came across someone perusing romance, I would engage them in conversation. Often, I would hand them a copy of my book and tell them I was in there for a book signing. The mere act of holding my book in their hand induced ownership and often, a sale would follow. But it wasn't so much about the sale, in the end it was about selling myself. It was about becoming a memorable author. If the person I was speaking to wasn't interested in romance, perhaps they had a friend who was. After that first signing, I realized that a successful book signing isn't having people lined up out the door, although if that were to happen, I'd be in book signing heaven! It's about getting your books in the store, having a place to sit and maybe, if you're lucky, having one person show up. That first book signing really helped to put this into perspective for me.

The Buddy System

Some authors like to have another person there signing with them so you don't have to sit there looking lost and lonely. I've done it both ways and they each have their merits. First of all, the buddy system will probably bring in more people since you are essentially doubling your publicizing efforts (or at least you should be). You can turn a simple book signing into an event. One of you can be having a book discussion or workshop, while the other author is signing. It's a great way to draw a crowd and keep a crowd. Also, often it's easier to get publicity when there's more than one author present. Unless, of course, you're Nora Roberts, in which case you can probably ignore the buddy system altogether. This type of book signing works well for unknown authors if you have a specific program or want to have a book signing that lasts all day.

No Sitting On The Job

As I mentioned previously, don't just sit there and smile. Get up, move around and engage people in conversation. Would you believe I've been told that some shoppers are actually intimidated to just walk up and talk to an author, but if you speak to them first you're breaking the ice and maybe, making a sale. Take your focus off of yourself and your stack of books and put it on the people in the store. As with anything in marketing you're really selling yourself and trying to focus on people in the process. Try getting up from your chair to greet people as they enter the store. I usually have a small flyer made up with the cover of my book, a blurb about it and I tell people I'm signing books today. Smile and talk to them and hand them a book. Begin to tell about your novel. Get them excited about it—let your passion shine through. Passion is a very contagious thing. People want to feel that same passion and folks love being around passionate people.

See What the Competition is Doing

Have you ever visited someone else's book signing? I did once and I felt like everyone there knew what I was up to. I wanted to see what it was about, to see what other authors did. Some of your best ideas or taboos will come from watching other people. I remember the first one I went to, I entered the store and there she was, the smiling author, pen ready and stack of books looming over the table. I wondered if I were just a customer that happened into the store, what would make me walk up to her unless my specific purpose had been to attend this signing? Then, I wondered what I could do to draw that traffic. Face it, no matter how much publicizing you do, unless you've got a spot on *Good Morning America* to talk up your signing, most of your foot traffic will probably just be shoppers. If you're really lucky you'll see some frantic people in search of last minute gifts (autographed books make great presents).

If you want to pick up tips from the pros, you might try visiting a celebrity signing or two. Check out: www.geocities.com/hollywood/hills/8944/.

They've got a frequently updated list of celebrities and well-known authors doing the book thing around town. Another great place is: www.publishersweekly.com/highway/index.asp. Both of these places offer a pretty complete listing. Publishers Weekly even separates them by author, state, book title or publisher. If you're going on the road for any reason, check out these sites and see if there's an event you can attend while you're away.

Be Unique!

If your book involves anything that you can tie in a theme or a prop, all the better. I went to a book signing for an author who specialized in period romance. This particular novel was set during the 1600's and she dressed in a gown fitting to the time. She also had a castle backdrop that a neighbor painted for her. Her neighbor was an aspiring artist, so not only was she doing the author a favor but the neighbor got to showcase her work as well. I have to tell you, people really love this kind of a thing. I mean anyone can sit at a table and smile, but sitting there in a corset for four hours takes real passion. So give some thought to what you can do to tie in a theme or prop into your signing. You don't necessarily have to show up in costume, but try to do what you can to set yourself apart from the rest. The important thing here is that while it's good to learn from the competition, you don't necessarily want to be exactly like them either.

Stuff To Do Before Your Book Signing

See if you can get a copy of the stores media list. More than likely the bookstore will send out press releases but it's important for you to do the same. Not only will you be able to target the same people twice, but the store manager will also know that you are actively involved in promoting your event.

Send a confirmation of your signing to the bookstore. They probably won't send it back but at least you can make sure they know where to get your book from and that you take your book signings very seriously. A sample of the form I use follows this chapter.

Start tapping into that media list you've been creating and begin contacting local media to promote your event.

Post your book signing information on the Author Appearances section of your web site.

Get invitations made up or make them yourself and send everyone on your contact list an invitation to your signing.

If you haven't already done so, get those bookmarks and postcards printed up. Don't forget to include the ISBN of your book, include a few review blurbs if you have them.

Get the cover of your book enlarged to poster size. Then, get it laminated and mounted. I had three of them printed up. I will usually drop one or two off at the store prior to the event so they can set them out and I'll bring the third one with me that day. Prop a sign up on an easel by the front door (where you will be standing and greeting people).

Dorothy Jane Mills, (DorothyJaneMills.com), author, editor and manuscript consultant, suggests getting colorful pens made up with the title of the book and author's name imprinted on it. When she does a book signing for her recent release, *The Sceptre*, she signs the book with one of her pens and lets the reader take it home with the book. Great idea and another nice way to spread the word.

Get signs made that say: "Book Signing Today" or "Author Appearance" both of these will help to draw crowds to your table.

Things To Bring To Your Book Signing

Bookmarks—I try to hand these out like crazy. Sometimes I'll even hand them out with the flyer when people enter the store. I've even autographed one or two when people hesitate to buy a book. More often than not, they return at a later time to buy a copy just because I gave them a bookmark.

Postcards—bring postcards with your book cover on them. I always say you can never have too many marketing materials.

Chocolate—I like to fill an attractive jar with Hershey's kisses or some other small chocolate. Food attracts people and may even keep them lingering a bit longer.

Guestbook—I always have people sign in at the event. If they give you their E-mail address inquire as to whether you can add them to your mailing list. This is a great way to build a "fan club" and continue spreading the word about your book as well as future novels. If you don't feel comfortable with a guest book, try putting together a free drawing. Tell them they don't have to be present to win. People hate that; I know I do. I mean who wants to stick around a book signing for four hours? Well, okay, except for the author. You should do what you can to keep a log of people that purchased your book. It's a great way to build your mailing list and customer base.

Make up a small flyer to hand to people who enter the store. They may not even know about your signing but you'll be sure to tell them. Keep in mind that heavy promotion of your book signing does not just benefit you, it also benefits the store and sends a strong message that you know how to move your books.

Your favorite pen.

During Your Signing

- Don't sit down unless you have to.
- Smile, talk and most of all have fun! This is no time to be shy.
- If no one shows up, remember, that's okay. It has happened to all of us at one time or another.
- Get people to enter your contest or sign your guest book.
- Tell the store manager that you'd like to sign the remaining books before you leave the store and see if they have "Autographed by Author" stickers for them. If they don't, you might want to think about ordering some from the American Booksellers Association (www.bookweb.org). You can get these and a variety of other book stickers for $5 a roll. These stickers will really help to move your book.
- Don't feel confined to stay just a few hours. Stay as long as there is an interest in the book. Once, I had a signing for two hours; I ended up staying for five.

What To Do After Your Book Signing

Send a thank you note to the person in charge of coordinating your signing. Don't send an E-mail; send a handwritten note. It will go a lot further!

A Few Final Notes

Be cautious of pay periods when scheduling a date for your signing. For example, I will always try to schedule mine around the 15th or 30th of the month. I live in a Navy town and since they never fail to get paid on those dates, it really helps to boost my sales. Also, check to see if the store has a newsletter. If it does, offer to write a short article on your book or discussion topic that will draw more attention to your signing. Keep the article interesting and helpful without giving away everything you plan to share with your guests. Or, if your book is fiction, share an interesting excerpt from it. Sometimes bookstore newsletters are printed by their corporate offices but generally they print them in-house and are always in need of "filler" items. Call your local TV stations and speak to the News Director. Call the day before (if your signing is on Sunday call them on Friday) and let him know you've sent a press release regarding your signing (you have haven't you?). If they need a sixty-second filler, you can offer their viewers some helpful tips on XYZ. Or, if your book is fiction, play up the "local author makes big" angle. Local stations love that. Speaking of media…If you can get yourself booked on a radio show the day before or preferably the morning of your signing you'll really help to boost interest. If you get some on-air time, consider giving away a few of your books during the show. Also check the book section of your local newspaper. Often, they will announce author events. Be sure to send them a notice of your event at least a month out.

Send a quick confirmation letter when you do get a book signing. It's shows your professionalism and lets the store know you're serious about this. Here's a sample of how one should look. Feel free to vary these depending on your book and the store.

*** Always send two copies of this form and an SASE to the Store Manager or Community Relations Manager the day you get confirmation of this event. ***

XYZ Bookstore
123 Elm Street
San Diego, CA

Dear XYZ:

This letter is to confirm that Penny C. Sansevieri will be doing a signing on November 25, 2002 from 10 a.m. to 3 p.m. at the following address:

XYZ Bookstore
123 Elm Street
San Diego, CA
(list bookstore and address again in case one store books signings for all of their other locations)
The book featured will be:
Get Published Today!

This book can be ordered in advance from the publisher:
Infinity Publishing
(877) BUY-BOOK (always list the 800 number for ordering)
We suggest ordering a quantity of 20 books for this event.

Community Services Manager_______________________________
                              Jane Lane
              (always type their name under the signature line)
Date: _______________________________

Thank you again for booking this event. I know it will be a success. I will be contacting local media in the area to notify them of this event and will keep you posted on any media coverage scheduled. Please return this form in the postage paid envelope provided, at your earliest convenient time.

Sincerely,

Penny C. Sansevieri

Marketing Tip:

Ask your friends to call two libraries and two bookstores requesting your book. Ask them to do this at least once or twice a week. Bookstores might not order your book but when you come through their door armed with your media kit they will certainly know who you are. Then again, when customers start asking for books they have a funny way of suddenly appearing.

40

Book Tours

A typical book tour can cost a traditional publisher upwards of $60,000 and send an author into a whirlwind of appearances, ribbon cutting ceremonies and other celebrity-like events. Book tours, while a great idea, don't have to cost you your entire marketing budget and then some. For the on-line published author, a book tour should be carefully planned to last no more than a few days or a week at the very most. If you can step away from your life for longer than that, great. But more often than not, it's not feasible to be gone from your full-time activities for two to three months.

If you have a book and are trying to figure out where you should target your book signing, here are a few things to consider. First of all, it's great if you can visit your hometown and do a trek through some of the neighboring cities. People love it when one of their own has become "famous" and you'll soon begin to realize that once you've gotten published, people will immediately begin to believe that you're having lunch with the likes of Steven Spielberg and Diane Sawyer. So, I say go with it. No, don't lie about who you're dining with these days, but ride the wave of fame as long as it will carry you. Contact your local Chamber of

Promotional Tip:

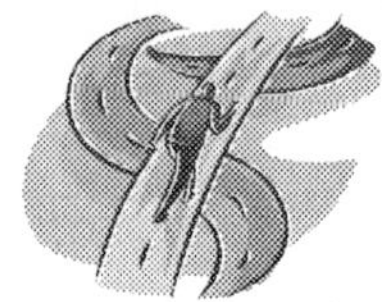

Going on the road? Don't forget to list yourself with "Authors on the Highway" at http://www.bookwire.com/highway/. This site is viewed by both the general public as well as industry professionals.

Also, don't forget to add your listing to Book Magazine's calendar section. Take a look at how their events are featured by heading over to www.bookmagazine.com and clicking on their "Calendar" section. Once you've done that you can send a quick e-mail to calendarlistings@ book magazine.com. It's a great way to get exposure.

Commerce, Kiwanis and Lion's Club organization. They're always looking for speakers. Get in touch with all of the bookstores in the area as well as libraries and schools. Let everyone know you're coming to town, I guarantee they will want to jump on the author tour bandwagon.

Another option for your book tour is the location where your story takes place. In *The Cliffhanger*, my love story happened in Newport, Oregon, in a fictional hotel called The Cliffhanger. It was a natural location for my first book tour. And I have to say, it was like a dream come true. I was headed up to Oregon to speak at a

Timing is everything

Most large publishing houses don't tour authors during the summer months (July & August). So if you want to book a tour, consider doing it then. A good advantage to this is that you can draw on the tourist traffic as well. Especially if you have a fiction book set in the town you're visiting.

Chamber of Commerce luncheon in the town of Newport where *The Cliffhanger* took place. I had even managed to schedule a few book signings and a radio interview. When one store couldn't schedule me for a signing, I offered to come in and sign their stock of books anyway (remember that "Autographed by Author" sticker). It was an amazing time and I am truly grateful to the people of Newport, Oregon for opening their doors to me.

Don't feel pressured to do an author tour. Certainly, if you can afford them they're a great way to get the word out about your books. If you need to cut expensive travel costs, do what Bobbie Christensen does on her trips. She tours in her RV and stays in KOA campgrounds for $20 a night. Sure, it might not be the most glamorous way to do your first tour, but you could probably visit more spots this way.

Whatever you decide to do, author tours can be great but exhausting. The first one I did, I ended up back at work the day after I returned and had to leave early because I was so tired. Don't be an over-achiever like me; take a day off before returning to your full-time job. Once you've done your first book signing you will know what I mean. An afternoon in the store, smiling and talking and being a perfect hostess, really takes it out of you. Then take that and times it by fifty and you've got a general idea of how tired you're going to be.

41

A World Of Thanks

One of the best ways to build relationships is to remember to thank people. I personally send thank you notes all the time. I send them after an interview. I send them to a media person who was considering my story but decided to postpone it for a while: "Thanks for taking the time to consider XYZ." I send one to the bookstore that hosted my signing. I even send it to the people that say "no". Thank them for taking the time to speak with you and thank them for considering your story idea, event or whatever it was you were pitching them. Trust me, they will remember you. Send them a card, not an E-mail. Preferably send them a postcard with your book cover on the front and a handwritten thank you note on the back. Think about it this way. You buy your neighbor's son a gift for graduation. He doesn't send a thank you note. When he gets married, you get him a gift as well. Again, you're ignored. Now, when that baby shower comes around what do you think you'll be getting them? You got it. It works the same in business. We're so busy and caught up in our lives and our own plans that we often forget to thank those people who are just as busy as we are and still took the time to listen to us. Remember, you need them more than they need you. So when you're putting together your marketing plan, add "send thank-you notes" to your list. I guarantee you won't be disappointed by the results.

42

A Few Final Words

Success comes in all shapes and sizes. For some, it's finally getting national media recognition, for others it's holding their finished book in their hand. But moreover, it's making a difference. When you get discouraged and when nothing seems to be working, remember why you got into this business in the first place. I don't mean to sound like Pollyanna about this, but there were days when all that got me through was a commitment I made to myself long ago. I used to say that if I could transport one person for an hour or two out of their own life and maybe help them in some way or allow them to forget their own worries, then I have achieved my goal.

Everyone who realizes they have literary blood coursing through their veins knows the passion that is at times all consuming. The on-line publishers understand this and know that what they have seen so far is only the tip of the iceberg. We are the trendsetters for the future. We are erasing old boundaries and delving into areas that were once off-limits to us. Whatever you choose to do with this information, know this: you have, right now, the opportunity to change or enhance someone's life. It is a gift that cannot and should not be ignored. It may not be something you do now, but know that the author in you will always try to come out. It is a voice that will never be silenced.

Becoming an author is not really a profession you choose, but rather it chooses you. There are days when I wish I did not have to write, some days it's more like a curse than anything else. But when we put pen to paper and the words seduce us into writing more, there's nothing else in the world like it.

Success Stories

"My first book signing was wonderful, it lasted over two hours and I was shocked by all the people that came to it. It was so incredible, I can't tell you how happy I was! Borders even bought eight of my books after the signing and placed them on the romance shelf. It brought tears to my eyes to see my books right beside those of Danielle Steele!"

Pamela Waller, *Treasure My Heart*

Sonia Pressman Fuentes was born in Berlin, Germany and came to the US as a child with her immediate family to escape the Holocaust. Her memoirs reveal how this five-year-old immigrant in 1934 grew up to become the first woman attorney in the Office of the General Counsel at the Equal Employment Opportunity Commission (EEOC) in 1965, one of the founders of the National Organization for Women (NOW) in 1966, the highest-paid woman at the headquarters of two multinational corporations—GTE and TRW, and an international speaker on women's rights for the US Information Agency.

"A world died when my parents died. I did not want that world to disappear without a trace. I did not want my own life to disappear either. And so, I wrote a book about their world and mine."

On the rewards of self-publishing her book, Ms. Fuentes has the following to say:

"There have been many exciting developments since I first published. Reviews have been glowing and there have been a good number of newspaper interviews. I receive an ever-increasing number of requests to do speaking engagements and memoir readings. This past March, I was one of five women in the state of Maryland inducted into the Maryland Women's Hall of Fame in Annapolis, Maryland. My memoir was used as a textbook at Cornell University in the Spring 2000 semester and is being used as a textbook in the Spring 2001 semester at American University in Washington, D.C. *Eat First—You Don't Know What They'll Give You, The Adventures of an Immigrant Family and Their Feminist Daughter* has been published in the U.K. and will be published in Russian by Planetree Publishing Ltd. and is in development as a stage play. My book and I were the cover story of the October 2000 issue of the Senior Beacon, a newspaper read by 200,000 seniors in Washington, D.C., Maryland, and Virginia. From a very shaky beginning as a retiree, I have entered upon the richest phase of my life."

Sonia Pressman Fuentes, *Eat First—You Don't Know What They'll Give You, The Adventures of an Immigrant Family and Their Feminist Daughter*
http://www.erraticimpact.com/fuentes

Ever heard of a little book called *The One-Minute Manager?* Ken Blanchard and Spencer Johnson originally self-published this book and decided to sell it for $15.00. Everyone cautioned them against selling the book at such a high price. Despite the nay-sayers, they sold over 20,000 copies of this book within three months the San Diego area alone.

They soon sold the reprint rights to William Morrow. *The One-Minute Manager* has been translated into over 25 languages and sold more than 12 million copies since 1982.

"I think the thing that pleases me most about being published is actually seeing my novel in the major bookstores. It was also very pleasing to be interviewed by the local television stations, having the opportunity to showcase my novel."

Will J. Sims, Brotherly Love

"Perhaps so far the greatest success is the Doubleday Broadway Books publication of the revised edition on December 26, 2000. The publicity has been great so far, The Early Show, Inside Edition, great print and radio publicity. But really my greatest satisfaction is when I hear from people who have read the book and have found and married their soul mates. One of the most exciting moments was when I got a contract from Random House (Broadway Books). But two others (in addition to the great publicity) were when I saw my name on the book when published by Xlibris and when I won the Colorado Independent Publishers Association (CIPA) Award in 1999."

Aggie Jordan, Ph.D., The Marriage Plan: How To Marry Your Soul Mate in One Year or Less,Broadway Books, New York (2000). www.themarriageplan.com

Janet Elaine Smith authored a book called *Dunnottar*, a historical novel set in Scotland. "I wouldn't even consider publishing traditionally. There's far more money in it doing it this way." I would tend to agree with her since she sold over 8,000 copies of *Dunnottar* marketing this on her own. "It was ranked the most popular book in Scotland on Amazon.com out of 8,764 titles. And it remained there for over two months."

I had a terrific conversation with Janet and she shared the following story with me: "When *Dunnottar* came out, it met with rave reviews. But when *In St. Patrick's Custody* arrived on the scene, something completely unexpected happened. Since it was set at a homeless shelter, I began to get e-mail from all over the country from people who had been inspired by the book and were turning up at their local homeless shelters to volunteer their services. The director of a homeless shelter from somewhere in Tennessee wrote me the following: "Three little old ladies came in one day, a copy of your book, *In St. Patrick's Custody*, in their hands. They asked me if I would read it, which I did. I found it delightful and very true-to-life of a shelter. A few days later they came back and asked if I had read it. I said I had. Then they said they wanted to be my new Graces. I told them that Grace was hired, and we had nothing in the budget to hire them. They insisted they wanted to be Grace before she was hired; they wanted to be volunteers. I asked them what their names were and they popped up immediately with 'Grace 1, Grace 2, and Grace 3!' I cannot thank you enough."

Janet Elaine Smith, Dunnottar—*In St. Patrick's Custody*

The Celestine Prophecy was originally self-published. James Redfield sold over 80,000 copies of his from the trunk of his car and then sold the reprint rights to Warner Books for $800,000! The book has gone on to sell 5.5 million copies.

"Placing my book with iUniverse is the best thing that I've done for my writing career. I'm selling books, connecting with readers, getting good reviews and working on marketing and promoting my book over the Internet every day. It's exhilarating and has been a fantastic experience!"

Wendy Tokunaga, *No Kidding—A Novel*

"I am certain that there are many more successes surrounding *Beyond the Blues—Treating Depression One Day at a*

Time than I may presently realize, but there are a few obvious accomplishments that I cannot deny. First, the letters I have received from people telling me what a difference the book has made in their lives. I am humbled by these gracious words…words that serve to remind me of the real reason I wrote the book in the first place…to spare one person and his or her family the agony of a suicide…to let that be my outward sign of my inward desire to help in some small way…but, to let the glory be for that Great Spirit, for without, I surely would have already perished."

Edward F. Haas, *Beyond the Blues—*
Treating Depression One Day at a Time.

Helpful Advice

"Set realistic goals…if you achieve your simpler goals…then raise the bar. I am certainly guilty of harvesting illusions of grandeur in the early stages of my project. We all dream of the BIG TIME. Just remember; if your goal is to be on the bestseller's list, chances are you will fail to reach your goal. If you hope to be on Oprah, just remember that Oprah receives over 10,000 books per year…most from major publishers and agents with big fancy trappings and lots of clout…stay true to yourself!"

Edward F. Haas, *Beyond the Blues—*
Treating Depression One Day at a Time

"Unfortunately, print advertising—even targeted to those who would seem most interested in your book—is largely a waste of money. Concentrate on getting book reviews and news releases in publications that cater to the book's intended audience. Also, if your book is aimed at a specific audience, get speaking engagements at clubs and organizations that would have an interest, and sell books there. Most of my personal sales of "Bent Wings" have been after being a Guest Speaker at aviation groups. In summary, you must be a "shameless promoter" of your work of art."

Fred "Crash" Blechman,
Bent Wings—F4U Corsair Action &
Accidents:True Tales of Trial & Terror!
www.expage.com/bent wings and
www.xlibris.com/bentwings.html

"Buy books. If you don't know what the other people are reading, the chances of your book being published go down immensely. When your book comes out, those are the people who will make—or break—your book.

If you haven't already done so, acquaint yourself with the editors at regional magazines and newspapers. Offer to write for them—even if you don't get paid. When your book comes out, these people will go the extra mile (and beyond) to help make your book a success."

Janet Elaine Smith, *Dunnottar—*
In St. Patrick's Custody—A Christmas Dream

"Perseverance, perseverance, perseverance! It's easier to write a book than to sell a book in my estimation. My book is extremely well received amongst the 12—step recovery communities, so naturally I try to get it in the hands of 12-steppers. If you're self-published you don't have national distribution so you got to generate awareness more creatively. My book ties in well with the 12-step recovery process so that's where I want my book to succeed. Authors have to bear in mind a few things…first, 50% of all books are sold through national book retailers, which means 50% aren't. Second, it is natural to think, 'if only my book was in Borders it would succeed', which is a flat out myth. Instead of worrying about how to get your book into Borders…you

need to be more concerned about how to get it out of Borders. Have you ever been to Borders? Unless you are a re-
nowned author (by the way that's less than 1% of all
authors) your book, maybe two books if your lucky, is lost in
the sea of one-inch spines. Nope, I'm not interested in that
at all. It's all about point of contact, point of sale. You know
whom you wrote your book for…now market to those people directly. Why should Borders have all the fun anyhow?"

Edward F. Haas, *Beyond the Blues—*
Treating Depression One Day at a Time
www.treatingdepression.com/

43

Great Resources

- *Book Marketing Update*—by John Kremer. This newsletter comes out twice a month and while it seems a bit pricey at $197 a year, it's worth every penny. To order contact (610) 259-0707 ext 433
- *Publicity Hound Newsletter*—Joan Stewart at www.publictyhound.com She offers weekly tips and a bi-monthly newsletter that I highly recommend.
- *1001 Ways To Market Your Book* by John Kremer—This was the first book on marketing I ever read and I have to admit, it overwhelmed me. But, it is the industry bible for self-publishers. If you're going to dive into book marketing, read *Jump Start Your Book Sales* first to get your feet wet, then take on the 673 pages of advice by John Kremer.

Jump Start Your Book Sales by Marilyn & Tom Ross. To order call: (800) 331-8355 or access their web site at: www.spannet. org/cc

Web Links

* **Author Event Promotion**

  - Freelancewriting.com/newssyndicator.html—they will list your writing accomplishment, be it an upcoming event, or company announcement.
  - Bookzonepro.com/calendar is one of the net's largest searchable databases. A great place to add your event.
  - Publishersweekly.com—a great resource to list your author event or book tour. Here's the link for submitting your information:http://publishersweekly.reviewsnews.com /index.asp?layout=authorsMain
  - Netread.com—they have a database of upcoming events you can search as well as submit your own to their site. They also offer a lot of articles, helpful links and great information for anyone publishing and promoting their book.
  - Writerswrite.com/events—another great place to announce your event, it will appear in their newsletter which goes out to thousands of authors each week.
  - Going on the road? Don't forget to list yourself with "Authors on the Highway" at http://www.bookwire.com/ bookwire/NetRead/index.html. This site is viewed by both the general public as well as industry professionals.
  - Are you an expert? If you are, try getting a listing at Yearbook (www.yearbook.com), these books get mailed out to the media on a yearly basis. If they're ever in need of an expert and they find your listing in Yearbook, you might just get a call.

❧ On-Line Newsletters & E-mail Newsgroups

- Writing for Dollars: Wfd-subscribe@topica.com—get free tips and tricks for maximizing your marketing dollars.
- Stay current with news from the publishing industry as well as marketing ideas and tips in this free bi-weekly e-mail newsletter. To subscribe send an e-mail to: get-published-subscribe@topica.com
- This newsletter really keeps me motivated to market, market, market. John Kremer's *Book Marketing Tip of the Week.* For your free subscription, send an E-mail to johnkremer@bookmarket.com.
- Interested in joining a group of fellow print-on-demand authors? Then, I highly recommend you send an e-mail to the following address: new_publishing-subscribe@topica.com
- Writerswrite.com—subscribe to this newsletter and keep abreast of what events are upcoming in the world of writing.
- Bookflash.com—the BookFlash Bulletin is a free newsletter from Bookzone. It features helpful tips, links as well as breaking news from the publishing industry. Head over to www.bookflash.com to subscribe.
- One of the most helpful discussion lists I belong to is at www.publish-l.com. Peruse the web site and read (and adhere to) their guidelines. You won't regret becoming a member of this highly informative group of people. There's a wealth of knowledge here, and I can't tell you how much I've learned from these folks.
- To get some essential tips and tools for publishing professionals, send Amy an E-mail at amy@bookzone. com or visit their site at bookzonepro.com.
- WritersWeekly.com is a great site and offers a weekly newsletter. To subscribe send an E-mail to writemarkets-subscribe@egroups.com

- Looking for ways to successfully navigate your life as a writer? Try *The Daily Grind*, a bi-weekly newsletter providing insightful tips and news writers can use. Send an E-mail to CHDailyGrind-subscribe@topica.com
- Interested in swapping ideas with other authors in the midst of promoting their books? Send an e-mail to self-publishing-subscribe@yahoogroups.com
- Need empowerment? Don't we all. Try sending an E-mail message to: get-published-subscribe@yahoogroups.com. This is a group dedicated to inspiring and empowering authors to keep them on track. They also share tips, tricks and media contacts. Great site!
- For a very spirited exchange on the life of an author/shameless self-promoter check out: http://www.writers-bbs.com/inkspot/threads.cgi?forum=selfpublish, you can't help but learn something from all of these posts. Go ahead, post a question and see what happens. I dare you. While you're there, swing on by the self pub center (there's a link on the page) for a ton of useful information.
- The Idea Lady is a great newsletter (published on-line every Tuesday). Subscribe to this newsletter by going to Cathy Stucker's site at www.idealady.com or by sending an E-mail to ideasub@idealady.com.

❧ Publicity, Resources & Promotion

- Bookzone.com from weekly newsletters to tips and advice, this site will keep you busy for a while.
- Literary Leaps is a great place to list your book-related web site. Visit them at www.literaryleaps.com.
- Bookwire.com will really help keep you on top of what's going on in the industry. They offer a section for promotion, event listing and regular E-mail updates.

- BookZonePro.com is chock full of valuable (free) information and resources for authors. Some of the services they offer are: free calendar listings, informative articles, daily news, and a searchable services directories.
- Wordmuseum.com—is a great resource to list your book, purchase advertising or submit an author interview.
- Writershelpdesk.com—a very useful web site for authors, filled with links, reports and helpful advice.
- Bookweb.org/ ABA—Association of booksellers—great site to locate bookstores and media materials.
- Freelancewriting.com—this is a great source, not just for freelance writers.
- Bookmarket.com—this site by John Kremer is a cornucopia of information to get you started and keep you going.
- Sharpwriter.com—offers tons of great information for writers, including a dictionary (can't have too many of those), a quotation section and an information area on grammar and punctuation.
- Ideasiteforbusiness.com—chock full of great advice, although more general in nature, I always seem to come away with at least a grain of new information. Sometimes that's all it takes.
- Publishing.about.com—a great resource for authors and self publishers. There are literally hundreds of links upon links from book fairs to marketing tips for authors and everything in between. Don't miss out on this one.
- Dailyglobe.com/day2day.html—a great site to figure out PR tie-ins for specific dates. At this site you will find thousands of dates from which to choose.

Research Related Sites:

- For those statistic gurus, here's a web site for you: the US government stocks a great deal of statistical information both geographic as well as demographic in the following location: http://tier2.census.gov/dbappweb.htm. If you're up for the challenge, it's worth the trip.

- Libraryspot.com—great site for research!
- Findarticles.com—a vast archive of published articles you can search for free. I can't tell you how often I've used this site, and it's constantly updated.
- If you're looking for information relating to life in early America head on over to: www.earlyamerica.com—it's filled with all sort of links, photos, maps and essays detailing the life our forefathers led.
- Yourdictionary.com—an excellent collection of dictionary portals. This site offers links to a huge selection of language dictionaries, including dictionaries for rarer (vanishing) languages, a good selection of Native American language dictionaries, plus translation tools and grammar.
- Need a statistic? Try Internetstats.com. You ask them a question and a real person will E-mail you back.
- Refdesk.com—refers to itself as "The single best source for facts on the Net." There's an incredible list of dictionaries, almanacs, encyclopedias and much, much more. There's even an atomic clock, ooooooooh.

Give me a place to stand, and I will move the Earth.

❦ Archimedes, 235 BC

Index